2 EXTI vouchers FREE

Now that you are a FOODIE Square Guide owner, we know you are serious about your food, so register your details with us and we will send you **2 extra FOODIE vouchers** and our quarterley newsletter **ABSOLUTELY FREE**.

Just fill in your details below, tear this page out and send back to:
The Foodie Square Guide Ltd, 21 Hargreaves Nook, Blakelands, Milton Keynes MK14 5BS

First Name: .... **Surname**: ....

Address: ....

....

.... **Postcode**: ....

Email: ....

Tel: ....

If you would like to order extra copies of THE FOODIE Square Guide at **£5** each **(plus £2.30 p&p per book)** please send a cheque payable to THE FOODIE Square Guide Ltd and indicate how many copies you would like. Thank you.

Please send me [ ] copies. I enclose a cheque for [£]

Contents

To find an establishment, look for it's entry number on each page

entry no. name/vouchers accepted

eating out

1 Al Tamborista £5
41 Auberge du Lac
34 The Boot at Sarratt
38 The Bricklayers Arms £5
7 Brook Hall Cookery School 10%
12 The Bull Inn 10%
39 The Cabinet 10%
11 The Carriage House Restaurant £5
13 The Carrington Arms £5 10%
9 The Crooked Billet 10%
48 The Dining Room
21 Earls Restaurant £5
40 The Fox & Hounds
32 Galloways £5
33 The Green Man £5 10%
25 The Horse & Jockey
36 Just 32 10%
29 The Kings Head
28 Menzies Flitwick Manor £5 10%
10 Moore Place £5 10%
23 Moreteyne Manor 10%
45 Murrays £5 10%
15 The Nags Head £5
16 The Navigation
2 The Old Green Man £5
47 The Old Talbot 10%
6 The Old Thatched Inn £5 10%
26 Paris House
27 The Park Bedford £5
22 The Plough at Bolnhurst
8 The Plough at Simpson 10%
5 The Plough, Wavendon

entry no. name/vouchers accepted

18 Prego Restaurants
30 The Prince of Wales £5 10%
19 Rajdhani £5 10%
49 The Red Lion, East Haddon
46 The Red Lion, Brafield-on-the-Green £5
35 The Silver Cup
14 Spooners £5
24 St Helena Restaurant 10%
37 The Tewin Bury Restaurant £5
4 The Verney Arms £5
44 The Vine House Hotel & Restaurant £5
3 Vine The Wine Bar £5
20 Voongs £5
31 The White Hart, Flitton
11 The White Hart, Grafton Regis 10%
17 The White Hart, Sherington
43 The Wollaston Inn £5 10%
42 Zodiac Restaurant

behind the scenes

Chef Profiles and Recipes

fine foods & wines

60 Absolutely Chocolate
59 Aubergine Fine Foods
53 Battlers Green Farm
52 Best Butchers
58 Browns Farm Shop
63 Byrmans
56 Country House Fine Foods

entry no. name/vouchers accepted

55 Delicatessen Estrella
61 Frosts
50 Halibut
57 Padbury Meats
54 River Nene
62 Shires Spit Roast Catering Company
64 Slow Food
51 Waitrose

lifestyle

68 Bang & Olufsen
70 Baker Bros Jewellers
73 Central Leasing
65 Claydon House
71 G Casino
69 The Grove Independent School
67 Morgan Gilder
66 Oliver James
74 Paula Stevens
76 The Stables
72 Whittlebury Day Spa
75 ZSL Whipsnade Zoo

award & competition

Nominate your favourite restaurant for an award and you could win a meal for two. Plus, a competition to win a family ticket for Whipsnade.

vouchers

The all important vouchers for this year, find them at the back of the guide.

Key to symbols

Families welcome
Wheel chair access
Garden/patio area
Accommodation available

Extensive Wine List (30 or more)
Extensive wines by the glass (10 or more)
Real ale
Live music or entertainment

Smoking area provided
Chef profile
FT Fair Trade produce used where possible
O Organic produce used where possible

Average cost of 3 course meal without drinks

A £20 or below
B £20 - £25
C £25 - £30
D £30 - £35
E £35 - £40
F £40 or above

FOODIE reader recommended
£5 £5 off
10% 10% off
Free bottle of wine

THE FOODIE voucher symbols

Please check individual entries for which FOODIE vouchers are accepted and any establishment terms (terms and conditions apply)

Introduction

Welcome to the sixth edition of our humble guide. I am pleased to say that as well as presenting you with our regulars we have added several new restaurants as a direct result of your nominations.

We value your opinions both good and bad and thank all who report back to us with 'your favourite restaurants'. If you uncover a hidden gem of a restaurant then please let us know, that way you can be confident that only the very best are included within THE FOODIE Square Guide.

You will also notice that we have increased our 'Fine Foods & Wines' section to include a more diverse selection of the very best in food suppliers.

Whilst on this subject, keep an eye out next year for a brand new range of products prepared for you by local chefs: 'In The Kitchen with…' products will be available from local delis and will come to you with quality you can rely on.

Congratulations to the following restaurants who have each won THE FOODIE AWARD as a result of your votes: St Helena Restaurant (Bedfordshire), The Plough at Wavendon (Buckinghamshire), Just 32 (Hertfordshire) and Murrays (Northamptonshire).

All the nominations received were gathered together, the lucky winner receiving a meal for two (excluding drinks) at one of the four winning restaurants drawn first. Well done to Ms Lesley Godfrey from Northants who wins a meal for two at the wonderful restaurant, "The Plough, Wavendon".

Don't forget to register to receive our FREE quarterly newsletter: *"Season"*, just tear out and send the enclosed '2 extra vouchers' page, or email us at thefoodie@thesquareguide.co.uk and we will put a copy in the post to you.

If you prefer the paperless version you can download the pdf from our website: www.thesquareguide.co.uk.

Well, that's about it for now...
Happy eating!

Paul Allen
Editor

Foreword

by our guest Chef for this year
Stephen Bulmer

I'm delighted to join the talented chefs and food retailers in The Foodie Square Guide who share my passion for great food and produce.

We opened Brook Hall Cookery School in May 2007 to meet the growing demand from consumers to understand more about the food and produce available to them and how to create delicious dishes from it.

As our business has expanded to encompass evening 'restaurant' opening at Brook Hall event catering and retail, I'm overjoyed to hear of more and more people seeking out great food producers in our area.

As customers, we are ultimately in control of what we buy in our shops and eat in our restaurants. Improvements will only be made if those of us who are passionate about food vote with our wallets; whether by supporting individual growers, or seeking out committed chefs, or refusing to compromise on the quality and husbandry standards of the chickens we buy in the supermarket.

The Foodie Square Guide is a huge support in this venture, publicising the best restaurants and food retailers in our area and providing a forum for readers old and new to share their finds.

Stephen Bulmer
Chef Director,
Brook Hall Cookery School

Food for thought

"Rocketing prices of fuel and food are the penalties we have to pay for incompetent government. Unfortunately there is little that our rulers can do in the short term to ease the pain of the explosion in commodity prices.

Looking to the long term, the dynamism of markets will eventually solve the imbalance between demand and supply for commodities. Demand will soften as consumers find ways to economize and substitute. Supply will strengthen as producers expand to profit from higher prices." **Source: Martin Spring, Economist, writing in his monthly 'On Target' newsletter.**

To say we live in challenging times would be an understatement: from the widely perceived threat of terror, to the real challenge of putting bread on our table.

For those in the developing world, the latter is of a more immediate concern as food and fuel make up a higher proportion of the household budget. Instability, chaos and changing governments will become a way of life. And not just for them.

The hugely influential political movement, the green lobby, will no doubt influence this further: Some good, some bad and some plain indifferent.. On a day to day basis – or a hand to mouth existence - this is going to be crucial.

Being part of a global economy and the huge impact that supermarkets have on our purchasing trends and habits, this does not bode well for the immediate to medium-term future.

Chefs have taken upon an almost 'rock-and-roll God' phenomenon, with many chefs who started out plying their trade, earning more than some musicians earn in a lifetime. And their opinions are becoming noticed, valued and used greatly.

Celebrity is a buzzword; higher food and fuel prices will still make the headlines and most importantly, the consumer of food – you and me – will be feeling the effects of an ever changing and evolving society.

Does that mean that we are doomed to accept a life of mediocrity and high prices in a time of recession? No. Simply put.

Britons tend to travel more than they did 15 or 20 years ago. In doing so, they have exposed their palates to a wider variety of cuisines and quality of food: from the humble market stalls in Africa, to the finest 3 Michelin-starred places in Japan, America and Europe.

As a result, we have become more discerning in our experiences and tastes: a R20 hamburger in a market in South Africa compared with a $200 meal in a restaurant in California, along with a £700 monthly food bill for home will have differing 'expected values'.

Joe-public is waking up to the reality of the cost of a carrot or potato.

Foodies, the world over, have embraced the dichotomy between real and perceived, yet have managed to get by: simply by being more discerning.

A farmer will not be able to sell his mediocre goods if a superior alternative can be sourced elsewhere – be that locally; nationally or internationally. Conversely, if a farmer has superior goods, we should be supporting him or her in their endeavours. Even in the short term, to allow him to grow and develop.

With this in mind, supporting our local economy becomes something of a 'given'. Farmer's Markets are 'de rigueur'. Sustainability, food miles and climate change all are on the politician's lips: That is big business to them – though they represent us, in business.

Compromising standards will only lead to a poor result. The best a chef can hope to achieve out of using mediocre ingredients.. Will be mediocrity. No matter the skills.

These recessionary times are exciting from a culinary perspective: The food issue is on everyone's lips. Even if it means sustenance or a way of venting about the value of a restaurant.

Turning a pig's ear into a silk purse is beyond most alchemists – though from a culinary perspective, a revival into the traditional methods of production and disbursement and in turn, consumption, a form of 'al Ancienne' is occurring.

Getting back to basics is no longer a trend, but a 'must-have'. From the simple 'grow your own' to the elaborate 'We have a bar and serve food' – both will have the urge to survive. It is instinct and something primal in our make-up, kicks in, to give us the impetus needed.

We all need to eat. It is a basic need – one of Maslow's magnificent seven.

How we choose to eat is governed by our hunger for nutrition: I choose a 'Live to eat' philosophy – and I'm particular in where I am able to source my produce from as it has a direct impact on my future health and well-being. Cost sometimes becomes irrelevant when weighing up the basics.

On your culinary journey, I wish you well. In discovering those hidden gems on your doorstep; the local produce from the farmer down the road and the pride you feel in buying local, supporting the local economy whilst becoming sated with the most wondrous of experiences in life, food.

It is essential in maintaining life.

It is crucial in its continued evolvement as a commodity we have got to rely on for sustenance and enjoyment. Even if the world is going to hell in a basket...

Grant Hawthorne
Head Chef
The Plough, Wavendon, Milton Keynes, Bucks.

eating out

eating out

Al Tamborista

Finest Italian & Seafood Cuisine

94 High Street
Stony Stratford
Milton Keynes
MK11 1AH
Tel: 01908 262632
Fax: 01908 260646
Email: info@hoteldifferentdrummer.co.uk
www.hoteldifferentdrummer.co.uk

FOODIE
Reader Comment

"The best Italian food for miles - with friendly service"
K. Pennington

The Al Tamborista restaurant where Old English hospitality meets Italian cuisine at its finest. Dinner is a relaxed affair, offering generous portions, imaginative sauces, 'al-dente' pasta and of course meat, fish, poultry and game to the highest standards.

The oak panelled dining room offers a burnished and welcoming glow to the guests, with sunlight streaming in during the day and a warm comfortable, candle-lit ambience at night.

The elegant stone street façade remains unchanged from 1743; a side entrance where the horses were stabled and the creaking coach put to rest for the night is still there, but inside light, warmth and comfort are better than they have ever been.

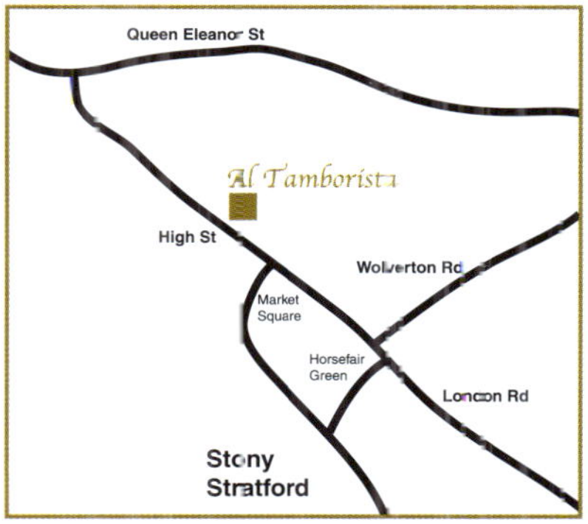

After your meal enjoy the comforts of the Hotel Different Drummer where the bedrooms have been redesigned with the modern traveller in mind. As well as all the practical accoutrements, they have been decorated with a sympathetic eye to the building's history; elegant antique furniture sits side-by-side with modern conveniences.

A warm traditional welcome awaits you.

Food served times:
Tue-Sat 12.00 noon - 2.30 pm & 7.00 pm - 10.00 pm

£5

Voucher accepted Mon-Thurs (3 course dinner only)
N.B. VOUCHER NOT ACCEPTED LUNCHTIMES

FT O lunch C dinner F

The Old Green Man

Country Pub & Restaurant

Watling Street
Little Brickhill
Milton Keynes
MK17 9LU
Tel: 01525 261253
Fax: 01525 261607
Email: info@oldgreenman.com
www.oldgreenman.com

FOODIE
Reader Comment

"Lovely modern place, cosy, extremely friendly, lots of food for the money"

R. Dean

The OGM continues to welcome you with friendly faces, delicious food and well kept ales.

Conveniently located in Little Brickhill, the OGM is just a few minutes from central Milton Keynes. With ample parking and easy access to the A5, we are the perfect destination for any occasion.

From light lunches to celebratory dinners, the OGM has something to offer everyone.......at any time. Our freshly prepared menu delivers quality and value for money; using the best of seasonal ingredients to recreate traditional favourites as well as contemporary British fayre.

Accompanying the great food, you will find an excellent selection of traditional ales, fresh sparkling lagers and ciders, plus a range of fine wines from around the world – many available by the glass.

Whether in for a meal or just a drink, the OGM welcomes you with open arms...we look forward to seeing you soon.

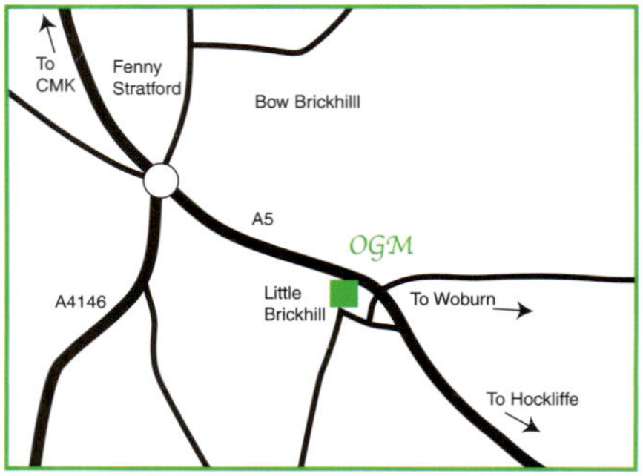

Food served times:
Mon-Fri 12.00 pm - 3.00 pm & 6.00 pm - 9.30 pm
Sat 12.00 pm - 5.00 pm & 6.00 pm - 9.30 pm
Sun 12.00 pm - 9.00 pm
Bookings advisable

£5
Vouchers accepted
Monday - Thursday only

FT O B

wine
the wine bar

92 High Street
Stony Stratford
Milton Keynes
MK11 1AH
Tel: 01908 566522
Fax: 01908 260646
Email: info@hoteldifferentdrummer.co.uk
www.hoteldifferentdrummer.co.uk

AA
One AA rosette for fine food

FOODIE
Reader Comment

"Fabulous food in a very nice atmosphere"
J. Sanders

Finding somewhere new, with a relaxed atmosphere and great food is not always easy. The Vine at Stony Stratford is just the place.

Located on the High Street a peep through the window will reveal a cosy wine bar and restaurant. Candles lighting the old stone fireplace with comfy sofas gathered around. A light wooden floor complements the chrome and brown contemporary furniture. A delightful mix of old and new, with an intimate bar at the rear. The temptation is to go inside.

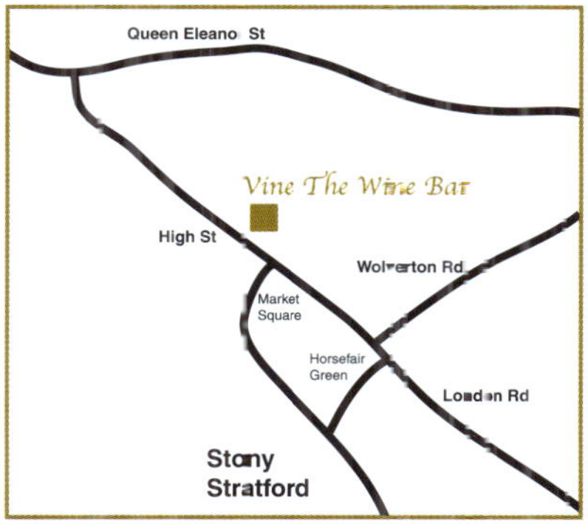

Warm, friendly staff will anticipate your every need, complemented with superb international cuisine and the finest selection of wines. Stylish music creates a background for elegant relaxed chic.

Vine believes in finest quality foods, beautifully presented for your enjoyment.

Food served times:
Mon-Sat 12.00 pm - 3.00 pm & 7.00 pm - 10.00 pm

£5

Voucher accepted Mon-Thurs (3 course dinner only)
N.B. VOUCHER NOT ACCEPTED LUNCHTIMES

THE VERNEY ARMS

GRATUS AD ORIS

Verney Junction
Nr Winslow
Buckingham
MK18 2JZ
Tel: 01296 712784
Email: info@theverneyarms.co.uk
www.theverneyarms.co.uk

FOODIE
Reader Comment

"Superb dinner - wonderful tender rack of lamb and fine vegetables."

S. Millichip

No more than a few minutes drive from the market town of Winslow, at Verney Junction; you'll find a real gem in the heart of the countryside - The Verney Arms.

Here you'll discover an amazing dedication to the Chef's Art, together with brilliant service in a refined and elegant atmosphere.

Karen and Lee pride themselves on knowing exactly what their diners expect. Lee has a natural passion for quality food, combined with Karen's attention to detail front of house, ensuring their increasing reputation for fine dining continues.

The Tapas Lunch Menu offers a variety of dishes to enjoy, while the evening, à la carte menu changes monthly, with emphasis on using only the finest ingredients to achieve the highest quality every time. And this really is what distinguishes this restaurant from the ordinary; consistently serving excellently cooked fresh food to charm and delight the discerning palate.

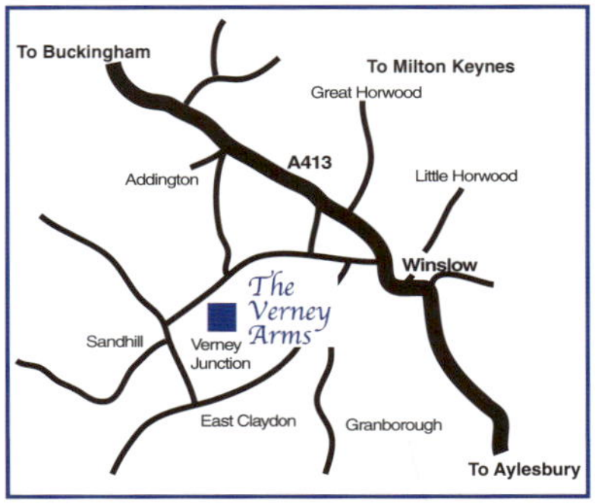

The restaurant has a wonderful feel to it, providing a unique ambience for a truly fine dining experience.

£5

Food served times:
Tue-Sat 12.00 pm - 2.00 pm & 7.00 pm - 9.30 pm
Sun 12.00 pm - 3.00 pm
1st Sunday of the month - Sunday Lunch Society

THE PLOUGH

72 Walton Road, Wavendon, Milton Keynes, Bucks MK17 8LW
Tel: 01908 587576
Email: reservations@theploughwavendon.com
www.theploughwavendon.com

FOODIE *Reader Comment*

"Absolutely fantastic dining experience from start to finish!!"
M. Davies

The Plough features contemporary furnishings, award winning wines, local and seasonal produce with a French/European influence and an award-winning garden area designed by the local Hasmead group.

On the site of the former 16th century Coaching Inn and old bake house, The Plough has been transformed into an elegant restaurant with bar facilities with a secluded garden courtyard for al fresco dining.

THE FOODIE AWARD 2008 Buckinghamshire winner
as voted by THE FOODIE Square Guide readers

The cuisine is where tradition meets contemporary with the classics and comfort foods being prepared with attention to detail. The service is discreet, professional and sleek: Attentive and friendly without being overbearing. Complimentary travel in a luxury 8-seater Mercedes is available by prior arrangement.

The restaurant is situated in the small parish village of Wavendon, South East of Milton Keynes in Buckinghamshire, and within walking distance of the internationally renowned The Stables music and entertainment venue. It is also an easy journey, by car, from both the Woburn Golf club and the M1.

With close proximity to Central Milton Keynes along with national rail and local bus services, The Plough also offers ample parking facilities for those wishing to make the journey by car. From London Euston station it takes approximately 35 minutes by train and a further 15 minutes by car from the station.

Wavendon is also close to the quaint villages of Aspley Guise, Woburn and the town of Woburn Sands, along with the world-renowned Woburn Abbey and Woburn Safari Park.

For copies of the current menus, wine list and news, please see the website: www.theploughwavendon.com

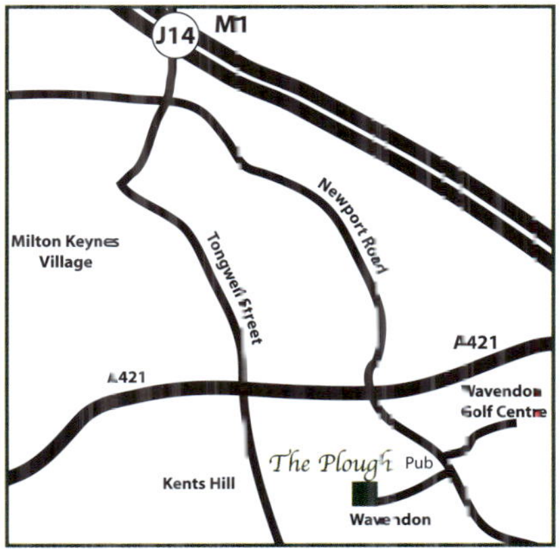

Food Served times:
Mon-Sat Lunch: 12.00 pm - 2.30 pm, Pre-theatre: 5.30 pm - 7.00 pm, Dinner 7.00 pm - 10.30 pm
Sun Lunch: 12.30 pm - 4.00 pm, Dinner: 7.00 pm - 9.30 pm

FT 0

The Old Thatched Inn

Main Street
Adstock
Buckinghamshire
MK18 2JN
Tel: 01296 712584
Fax: 01296 715375
Email: enquiries@theoldthatchedinn.co.uk
www.theoldthatchedinn.co.uk

The Old Thatched Inn sits quietly in the picturesque village of Adstock between the towns of Buckingham and Winslow. It was built in 1645 and first opened its doors to the local community in 1702.

Owner and ex-chef Andy Judge is a superb host, his experience ensuring that everything is done correctly. He has a great team that are both friendly and efficient. Whether you relax in the comfortable bar area where the traditional lunch and dinner menu are always available, together with a superb selection of quality wines, real ales, premium lagers and soft drinks; or you eat in the tastefully decorated conservatory restaurant, the attention to detail is the same. Renowned for serving fresh food, professionally prepared by his team of chefs, using local produce (whenever possible) and a superb range of prime cut meats and fresh fish.

With ample parking, splendid dining room and well-stocked bars, The Old Thatched Inn is the perfect venue for that special occasion, whether a wedding or birthday party.

FOODIE
Reader Comment

"Very welcoming and gorgeous food in a nice relaxed atmosphere"
A. Davies

Opening times: 12 noon - 11.00 pm
Food served: **Mon-Fri** 12 noon - 2.30 pm & 6.00 - 9.30 pm
Sat 12 noon - 9.30 pm
Sun 12 noon - 8.00 pm
Restaurant times may vary due to season

FT O

Vouchers valid Mon-Thurs from à la carte only
£5 10%

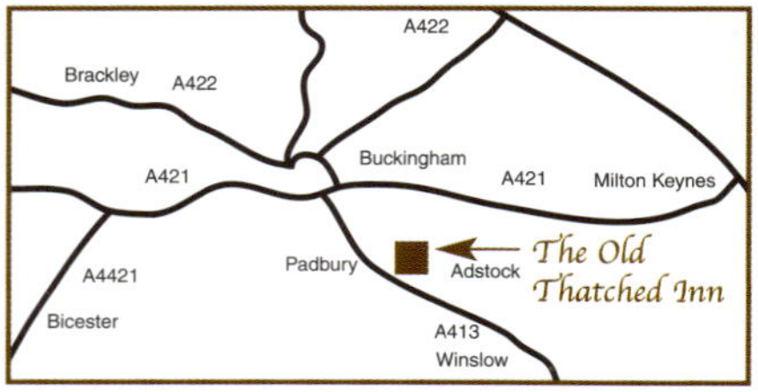

Brook Hall Cookery School

Brook Hall
9 Sheep Street
Winslow
MK18 3HL
Tel: 01296 712111
www.brookhall.net

Situated in the pretty market town of Winslow, Buckinghamshire, Brook Hall Cookery School offers one day cookery classes for amateur chefs of all ages and abilities – including children – across a wide range of subjects.

Brook Hall is owned and operated by Stephen Bulmer, who was previously Chef Director of the Raymond Blanc Cookery School at Le Manoir aux Quat'Saisons and has worked at top-level restaurants all over the world. Courses offered reflect Steve's breadth of experience and include Fish and Shellfish, Meat & Poultry, Flavours of the Orient, Italian Cookery, Game, Barbecuing and Seasonal Dinner Parties.

Dining at Brook Hall

Brook Hall is also open for dinner most Thursday – Saturday nights, plus some Sunday lunches. Meals are served 'table d'hote' style in Brook Hall's period dining room. Guests eat together at a single seating, around one large table, making for a convivial dining experience.

Stephen creates a different three course set menu each evening, priced at £28 per person (vegetarian and other special dietary requirements by prior arrangement). Wines are available from the wine list, or you can bring your own at £15/bottle corkage.

Once each month Brook Hall hold a special Gourmet Evening offering aperitif, four-course menu with accompanying wines and coffee, priced at £75 per person.

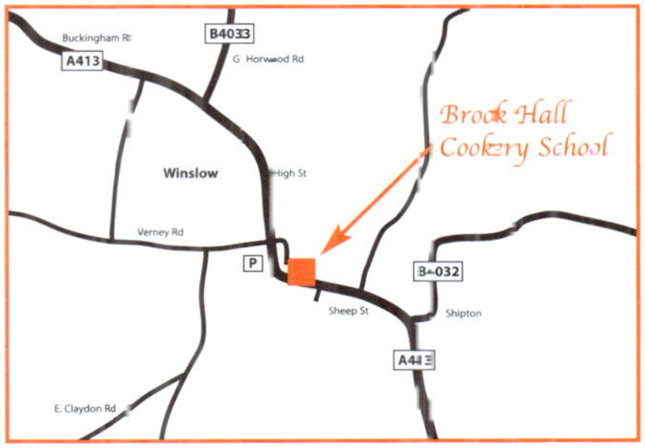

Dates and menus for all the above are published monthly on the Brook Hall website.

Private Dining, Outside Catering and Corporate Events

Brook Hall also offer private dining at Brook Hall, an outside catering service and corporate events/entertainment.

FT O 10%

THE PLOUGH *at Simpson*

Simpson Road, Simpson Village, Milton Keynes MK6 3AH
Tel: 01908 691555
Fax: 01908 696915
Email: theploughatsimpson@hotmail.com
www.theploughatsimpson.co.uk

FOODIE
Reader Comment

"Ian and Claire are excellent hosts and their chef Mark never fails to produce a fabulous meal"
D. Pittard

Winners of "Charles Wells Area Pub Of The Year 2007" this increasingly popular village pub has received a new lease of life over the past couple of years since owners Ian and Claire Estick arrived in 2004. Set in the old village of Simpson it is only 5 minutes from Central Milton Keynes but away from the hustle and bustle of the city centre on the banks of the Grand Union Canal.

This independent, family run pub and restaurant, offers a relaxing, friendly atmosphere with a great selection of fine wines, real ales and superb food prepared from the freshest ingredients.

With both traditional bar fare, à la carte dining with a wide range of weekly specials (and when the weather permits) canal side BBQ's you can find something on the menu to suit your mood. Their famous "Bulleit Bourbon" steak, fresh fish, poultry and far from boring vegetarian options, the menu mirrors the seasons to take full advantage of the best locally produced produce for the time of year.

Being independently owned The Plough has a reputation for offering excellent bespoke celebration menus and party venue for all budgets and occasions.

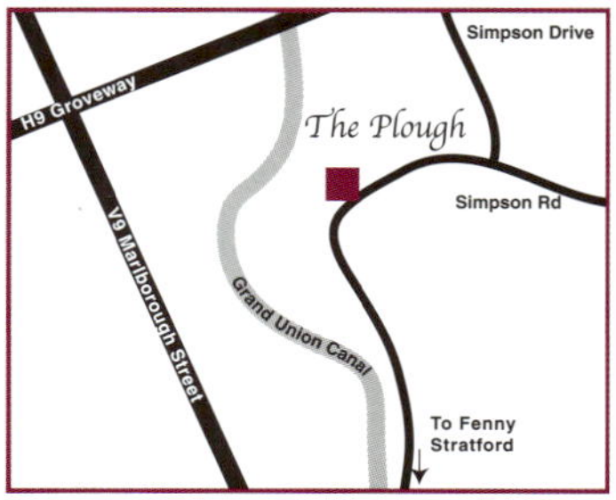

If you have not seen the transformation from the Si-Fi world of what used to be Trekkers to the now light, modern destination pub which is The Plough a visit is highly recommended. If you've experienced the welcome, quality of food and service recently we know you will be visiting again soon!!

Food served times:
Mon-Thur 12 noon - 2.15 pm & 6.00 pm - 9.30 pm
Fri-Sat 12 noon - 2.15 pm & 6.00 pm - 10.00 pm
Sun 12 noon - 4.00 pm

10% FT

The Crooked Billet

2 Westbrook End, Newton Longville, Bucks MK17 0DF
Tel: 01908 373936
Fax: 01908 631979
www.thebillet.co.uk

FOODIE *Reader Comment*

"Exceptional attention to detail without being obtrusive or pretentious. Delicious food and exceptional wines in a convivial setting" J. Lewandowski

"THE FOODIE Award 2007 - Bucks" - THE FOODIE Square Guide
"50 best restaurants in the UK" - The Independent Guide
"One of the best restaurants outside of London" - Tatler Guide
"Cheeseboard Of The Year 2003, 2004, 2005" - National Cheese Awards
"Gastro Pub Of The Year" - The Times
"Milton Keynes Restaurant Of The Year" - MK News

Recognised as one of the best Gastro Pubs in the UK - The Independent Guide, The Times and Square Meal Guide and voted "Best Restaurant 2007" by the readers of THE FOODIE Square Guide.

Local lamb, beef, pork, poultry and game. Lobster, scallops and langoustine from Scotland, Cromer crab, turbot, brill, seabass, hake, monkfish and cod from Cornwall & Devon and Norfolk asparagus, samphire and strawberries are just some of the ingredients on our menu.

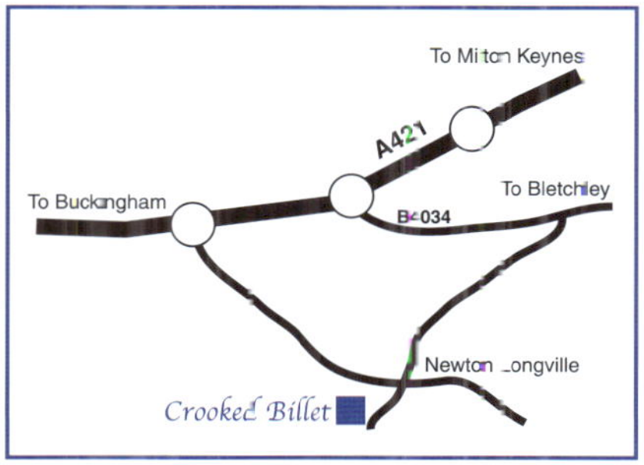

Food Served times:
Lunch - **Tues-Sat** 12 noon - 2.00 pm **Sun** 12.30 pm - 3.30 pm
Dinner - **Mon-Thurs** 7.00 pm - 9.30 pm **Fri-Sat** 7.00 pm - 10.00 pm

Vouchers valid Mon-Thur only
10%

FT O

Moore Place Hotel & Greenhouse Restaurant

The Square, Aspley Guise, Milton Keynes MK17 8DW
Tel: 01908 282000
Fax: 01908 281888
www.mooreplace.com

FOODIE
Reader Comment

"My favourite local restaurant"
M. Wood

Moore Place Hotel, an elegant Georgian mansion originally built by Francis Moore as a family home, is set in The Square of the tranquil and picturesque village of Aspley Guise in Bedfordshire.

The public areas are both spacious and comfortable and the Bar is a popular place for guests to gather.

The Greenhouse Restaurant is a light and airy Victorian style conservatory overlooking the rock garden, through which a water cascade falls into a lily pond below, complete with our collection of fish.

Clive Southgate, the Head Chef offers a subtle blend of traditional English and Continental cuisine, with produce from the local suppliers he can guarantee quality, accompanied with an extensive wine list. The emphasis is on an informal atmosphere with superb food and excellent wines. The Greenhouse Restaurant is perfect for that special celebration meal for two, entertaining business clients or for dining with your family and friends. We also have a variety of private rooms, ideal for that special occasion.

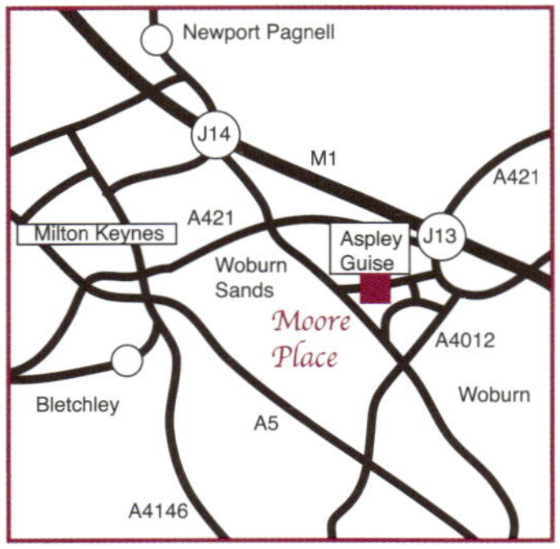

Why not come along to one of our famous 'Murder Mystery Nights' or contact us for a full calendar of events.

Food served times:
Mon-Fri 12.00 pm - 2.00 pm & 7.00 pm - 9.30 pm
Sat 7.00 pm - 9.30 pm
Sun 12.00 pm - 2.00 pm & 7.00 pm - 9.30 pm

£5 10%

The Carriage House Restaurant

Claydon House
Middle Claydon
Bucks
MK18 2EX
Tel: 01296 730004
Email: carriage.house@btconnect.com
www.thecarriagehouserestaurant.co.uk

Within the courtyard of the magnificent Claydon House Estate, you'll find The Carriage House Restaurant, offering you renowned cuisine surrounded by beautiful gardens and breathtaking parkland.

Following 15 exciting years running Oxfordshire's famous restaurant boat, "Rosamund The Fair", the owners, Tim Matthews and Sophia Goodford, have transformed the restaurant into an opulent dining room experience that's hard to resist.

Acclaimed Head Chef Jason Caple and his team use only the very best, carefully sourced produce, offering you beautiful modern British cuisine. The finest meats from local butchers, fresh game from the estate and seasonal fruit and vegetables from the kitchen garden are all used to create delicious and imaginative dishes for you to savour.

The menus change regularly with the restaurant open for fine dining on Friday and Saturday evenings, subject to availablity. On Sundays, you'll find indulgent two and three course lunches. Plus, if you're in the mood for something a little lighter, a mouth-watering lunch menu is served throughout the year.

The ideal venue for weddings, parties and corporate events, you can enjoy exclusive use of the restaurant any day of the week. A quiet, professional approach ensures your event is truly memorable.

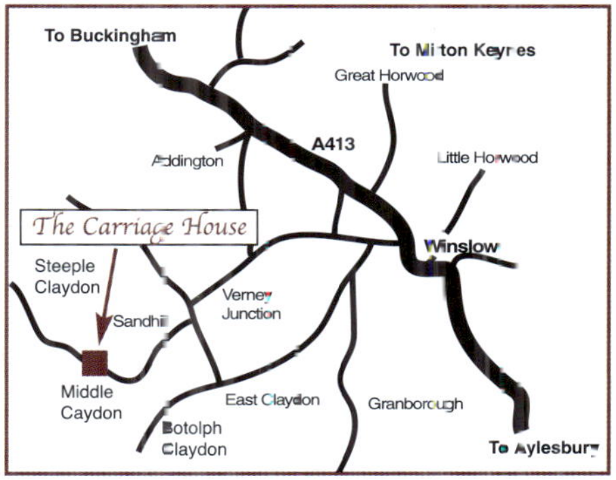

FOODIE
Reader Comment

"We had an amazing time and made even better because this was a surprise arranged by our friends. Will definitely be back again soon and will highly recommend to all" S. Wilding

Food served times:
Mon-Wed 12.00 pm - 3.00 pm
Thur Closed
Fri-Sat 12.00 pm - 3.00 pm & 7.00 pm - 9.30 pm
Sun 12.00 pm - 3.00 pm

£5

FT O Lunch B Dinner D

THE BULL INN

OLNEY

9 Market Place
Olney
Buckinghamshire
MK46 4EA
Tel: 01234 711470
Fax: 01234 241862
Email: thebullolney@gmail.com

FOODIE
Reader Comment

"Tasty, modern food in relaxed surroundings - very good."
S. Beaumont

Situated in the heart of Olney's market place is the 400 year old Bull Inn, formerly a coaching inn for the landed gentry. The Bulls character, warmth, friendly and professional service makes it a perfect venue for any occasion.

The Bull has a well earned reputation for well kept cask ales and is renowned for Sunday lunches in addition to a freshly prepared, varied menu which attracts visitors from all over the local area. Extensive gardens and walled courtyards make the Bull an ideal place to unwind and relax.

Our freshly prepared menu aims to provide simple, well cooked food, made from the best ingredients and sourced locally whenever possible.

The menu changes regularly to reflect the changing seasons and availability of fresh local produce.

The Bull's Function Suite caters for up to 80 people, and has its own access, bar and toilets. The room can be used for Training, Presentations, Conferences, Dinners or Parties.

Food served times:
Mon-Fri 12.00 pm - 2.30 pm & 6.00 pm - 9.30 pm
Sat 12.00 pm - 4.00 pm & 6.00 pm - 9.30 pm
Sun 12.00 pm - 4.00 pm

10%

FT O

The Carrington Arms

Cranfield Road
Moulsoe
Newport Pagnell
MK16 0HB
Tel: 01908 218050
Fax: 01908 217850
Email: carringtonarms@aol.com
www.thecarringtonarms.co.uk

FOODIE
Reader Comment

"Marvellous choice of food, well presented and very good service"
I. Webster

Now under new ownership and recently refurbished The Carrington Arms is an imposing 19th century listed building only one mile from junction fourteen of the M1 in the picturesque village of Moulsoe.

This award winning pub/restaurant probably has one of the largest selection of meats and fish on offer in the area. All are imaginatively displayed in a large chilled counter for you to choose, the selection includes; Prime Herefordshire Beef, quality Gloucester Old Spot Pork Sausages and Fresh Seafood. Everything is priced by weight. A good recommendation is The Carrington Arms famous "Bourbon Steak", marinated in Bourbon Whisky, black treacle, brown sugar and soy sauce. Your chosen meat is then cooked on an open char-grill within your view exactly to your liking. Choose from a selection of freshly prepared seasonal Modern British dishes such as Woburn Estate Venison with a Red Wine and Chocolate Sauce and a mouth-watering array of homemade desserts as well as a varied snack menu for those with less time.

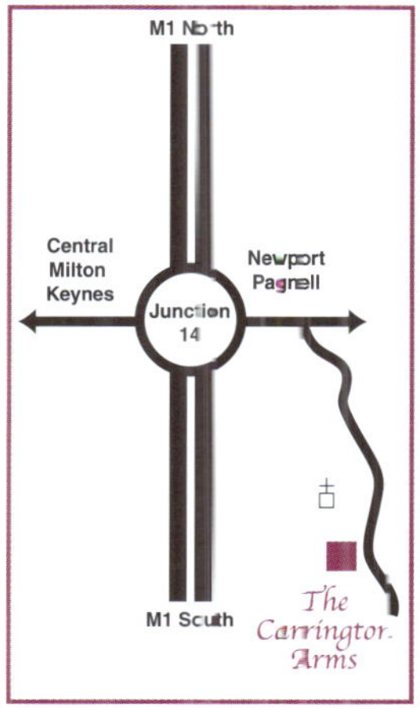

There are eight comfortable en-suite letting bedrooms and a premier suite within the gardens, each with tea and coffee making facilities and continental breakfast delivered to your room.

You can also drop in just for a drink, with an extensive range of wines, vintage whiskies and a great selection of real ales on offer. It's recommended to book your table if you intend to have a meal to avoid disappointment. There is ample parking on the gravel car park to the side of the restaurant.

Opening times:
Mon-Sat 12 noon - 3.00 pm & 5.30 pm - 11.00 pm
Sun 12 noon - 3.00 pm & 7.00 pm - 11.00 pm

Food served:
Mon-Fri 12 noon - 2.30 pm & 6.30 pm - 10.00 pm
Sat 12 noon - 2.30 pm & 6.00 pm - 10.00 pm
Sun 12 noon - 2.30 pm & 7.00 pm - 9.30 pm

£5 10%

Spooners

61 High Street, Woburn Sands, Milton Keynes MK17 8QY
Tel: 01908 584385
Fax: 01908 281405
Email: ray@spooners.co.uk
www.spooners.co.uk

Spooners Restaurant ~ simply unique

FOODIE
Reader Comment

"A refreshingly different restaurant serving an original menu with a warm welcome"

C. Watkins

Spooners restaurant was established over 25 years ago and is now in the very capable hands of husband and wife team Ray and Liudmila Ripnar.

Spooners has always had a firm reputation for presenting consistently high quality fresh food and famous locally for its celebrated Henry Marshall dish. Recognised for its consistent quality of fresh food, service and ambience it is a favourite destination for special occasions, parties and weddings.

Both Ray and Liudmilla are proud to continue this long-standing commitment to providing first class service in a relaxed setting. *"The menu will be regularly reviewed and developed in light of what you, the customers enjoy. We are maintaining the usual high quality of our menu. You may notice, however, a new and exciting Russian twist to some of the dishes. Recent customers have enjoyed and complimented on the fine exotic Russian cuisines which have been specially prepared by Liudmila and head chef, Vitaly"*, says Ray.

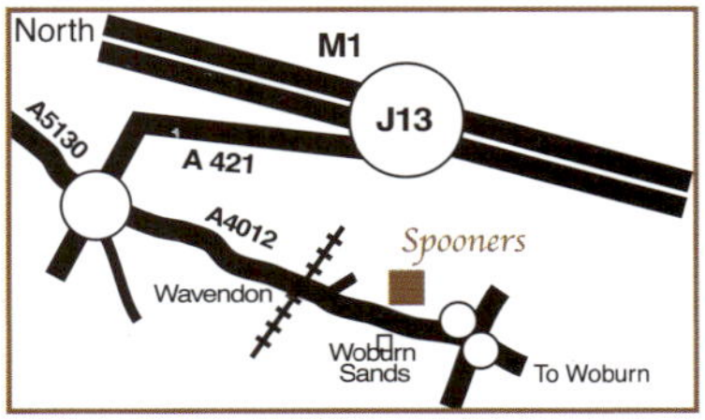

Vouchers accepted Tue-Thur only for Lunch and Dinner

£5

Opening times:
Tue-Sat 12.00 pm - 2.30 pm & 7.00 pm - 10.30 pm
Sun 12.00 pm - 2.30 pm

The Nags Head

London Road
Little Kingshill
Great Missenden
Bucks
HP16 0DG
Tel: 01494 862200
Fax: 01494 862945
Email: goodfood@nagsheadbucks.com
www.nagsheadbucks.co.uk

FOODIE
Reader Comment

"Delicious and different - definitely one of the finest restaurants in the area"
P. Wakefield

Alvin and Sally Michaels are proud to welcome you to The Nags Head in Great Missenden. Following three months of careful renovation, the Michaels family, owners of the award-winning Bricklayers Arms in Flaunden, Hertfordshire, invite you to experience at The Nags Head the same English and French fusion cooking that has won them so much recognition to date. From Duo of Pan-fried Foie Gras on Rocket and Foie Mi Cuit served with a Fig Chutney, Home Smoked Fish Selection, to Sliced Beef Tail Fillet of 21 Day Aged Beef served with a Mushroom Ducell and a Madeira Sauce, the menu offers a wide range of delicious dishes, freshly prepared by some of the country's leading chefs.

Food is their passion; they use only the finest organic produce available knowing that this really does make a difference and (wherever possible) sourced from local suppliers.

There is also an extensive wine list to suit all tastes and a selection of real local ales guaranteed to warm your palate.

And should you wish to extend your stay, why not retire to one of the seven double-bedrooms, each beautifully refurbished and equipped with shower ensuite.

After a rested night's sleep, you'll find a hearty breakfast waiting for you in the morning.

However long your stay at The Nags Head, your hosts do their best to ensure it'll be an experience you'll wish to repeat again and again.

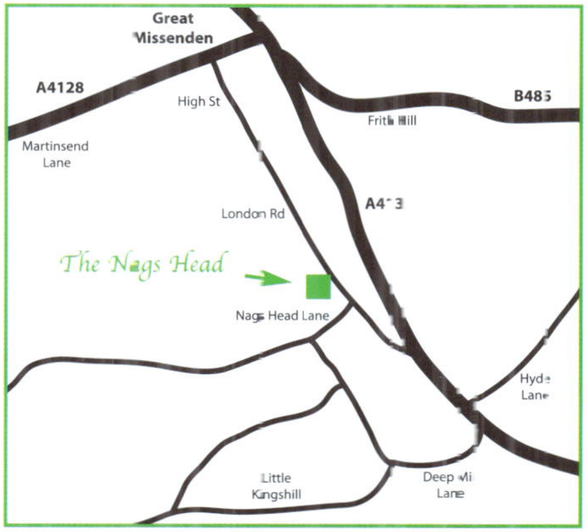

Food served times:
Mon-Sat 12.00 pm - 2.30 pm & 6.30 - 9.30 pm
Sun 12.00 pm - 3.30 pm

£5

FT O

The Navigation Inn

Castlethorpe Road
Cosgrove
Milton Keynes
MK19 7BE
Tel: 01908 543156

FOODIE
Reader Comment

"Great food, great staff and great location - Top marks!"
D. Crawley

The Navigation Inn is set alongside the Grand Union Canal at Cosgrove on the Castlethorpe Road only 10 minutes drive from Central Milton Keynes. It has arguably one of the best canal-side views in the area and is very much a traditional old style pub. Built 200 years ago alongside the opening of the canal it is well known locally and is extremely popular especially during summer weekends with customers coming from near and far to enjoy good food, real ale and the canal-side gardens. If the weather is kind there can be stunning senset views from the balcony as the sun drops slowly over the canal.

Now under new ownership and with the emphasis on fresh local produce, the menu is very much traditional pub fare but with some interesting additions courtesy of the owner's son and head chef Dan.

Friday evenings, usually around 8.30pm, The Navigation becomes a popular music venue with an exciting mix of bands, solos and duos. It is also a regular stop off point for business lunches and is renowned for its Sunday roasts.

In the winter months you can sit and relax in front of the open log fire and just take in the ambience.

Food served times:
Mon-Thur 12 noon - 2.30 pm & 6.00 pm - 9.00 pm
Fri-Sat 12 noon - 2.30 pm & 6.00 pm - 9.30 pm
Sun 12 noon - 5.00 pm
Summer: Fri-Sun 12 noon - 9.30 pm

The White Hart

1 Gun Lane
Sherington
Newport Pagnell
Bucks MK16 9PE
Tel: 01908 611953
Fax: 01908 618109
Email: whitehartresort@aol.com
www.whitehartsherington.com

THE WHITE HART
SHERINGTON

FOODIE
Reader Comment

"A lovely country pub with excellent home-cooked food and friendly service"

M. Simons

Gun Lane can be found just on the outskirts of the small hamlet of Sherington, only 10 minutes drive from the hustle and bustle of Central Milton Keynes. The White Hart is a picturesque 17th century freehouse, situated in the calm of the Buckinghamshire countryside.

Ideal for that relaxing drink and some quality time that you've been promising yourself. This tranquil inn can also offer to the weary traveller some superb accommodation in its beautifully converted barn.

You are assured of a warm and friendly welcome from staff that know what you expect. Whether it's a meal sat in the comfortable restaurant which supplies freshly prepared lunches and evening meals or if you would prefer, simple bar snacks and tapas to complement its fine selection of cask ales.

Voted CAMRA regional pub of the year 2002 and 2003; enjoy your favourite tipple in the beer garden or out on the large patio area.

English Tourism Council ◆◆◆◆ guest accommodation.

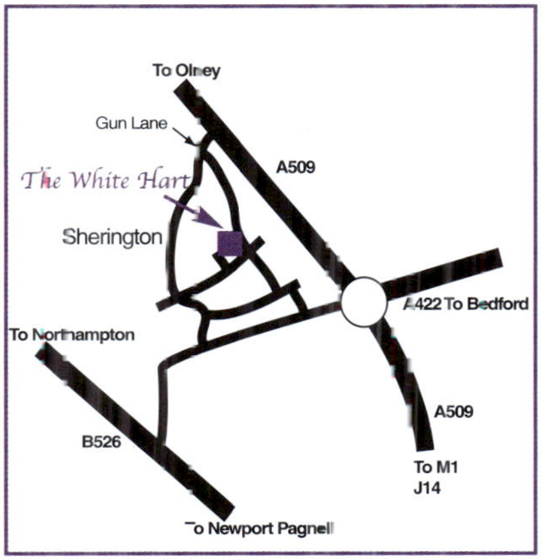

Opening times: 12.00 noon

Prego

4 High Street
Buckingham
MK18 1NT
Tel: 01280 821205

24-26 St Mary's Road
Market Harborough
LE16 7DU
Tel: 01858 469169

8 St John's Street
Newport Pagnell
MK16 0EP
Tel: 01908 217535

18 Bedford Street
Woburn
MK17 9QB
Opening October 2008

Email: mail@pregorestaurants.com
www.pregorestaurants.com

Mediterranean style restaurant and wine bar. Prego meaning 'you're welcome' offers you Mediterranean food with typically relaxed and friendly service in a lively atmosphere.

Our Italian influenced menu caters for all times of the day or just visit for a coffee or a drink. We offer an extensive choice of food which apart from the vast range of traditional Italian pizzas and pasta, offers a fantastic choice of fresh chicken and seafood dishes alongside tasty vegetarian options.

But don't forget to leave room for our delicious Mediterranean desserts which include traditional Italian ice creams and sorbets. Children are always welcome and catered for with our excellent children's menu.

We look forward to seeing you.

FOODIE
Reader Comment

"Informal and relaxed with delicious freshly made Italian food"
J. Moore

Opening times:
Mon-Sun All day from 10.00 am - 10.30 pm

Voucher valid Mon-Thurs only

Rajdhani

706 Midsummer Boulevard
Food Centre
Central Milton Keynes
MK9 3NT
Tel: 01908 392299
Fax: 01908 392541
www.rajdhanimk.com
Restaurant/Take-away

"As featured on BBC's Look East"

Situated next door to Waitrose in the food centre of Central Milton Keynes is "The Rajdhani Restaurant". This spacious restaurant which has been featured on the BBC's programme Look East is owned and run by a very convivial host Ali.

Having been voted one of the top 100 restaurants in The British Curry Awards on two occasions you can expect good food and excellent service.

The Rajdhani is a popular restaurant serving freshly prepared food. The team of chefs are justifiably proud of what they do. All dishes contain no artificial colourings, which will appeal to many.

There is a popular buffet all day Sunday and Monday evening where for £9.95 (half price for children) you can taste a selection of dishes, and with ample free parking it's perfect for that Indian meal that you've been promising yourself!

FOODIE
Reader Comment

"There are many Indian restaurants but some outshine the rest and this is definitely one of the finest"

K. Pennington

Opening times: Open 7 days a week
Mon-Thur 12 noon - 2.30 pm & 6.00 pm - 11.00 pm
Fri 6.00 pm - 12 midnight
Sat 12 noon - 2.30 pm & 6.00 pm - 12 midnight
Sun 12 noon - 10.30 pm

£5 10%

Voongs

1-2 Woodward House
Cambridge Street
Bletchley
MK2 2TH
Tel: 01908 370292

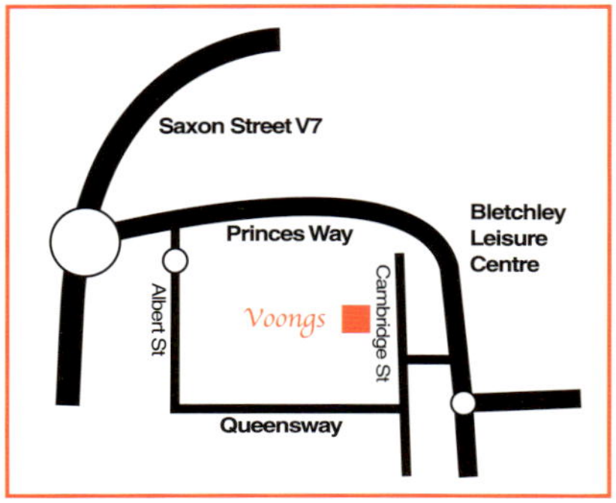

You must try it to believe it.

Opening times:
Mon-Fri 12 noon - 2.00 pm & 6.00 pm - 10.00 pm
Sat 6.00 pm - 10.00 pm
Sun 12 noon - 2.30 pm & 6.00 pm - 10.00 pm

£5

Earl's Restaurant

119 Dunstable Street, Ampthill, Bedfordshire MK45 2NG
Tel/Fax: 01525 404024
Email: earlsrestaurant@tiscali.co.uk
www.earlsofampthill.com

Situated in the Georgian market town of Ampthill, Earls Restaurant is an old Tudor building dating back to the 17th century. Earls has been carefully transformed into a stylish brasserie set over two floors. Modern design yet still retaining the old wooden beams and floors, Earls remains one of Bedfordshires most popular eateries. Established in 1999 the restaurant serves English/French cuisine.

Head chef Nicole who has 20 years experience cooking in many award winning country hotels and restaurants has over the years achieved a standard of 2AA Rosette cooking. Using local and seasonal produce is an important factor to the continued success of Earls. The menu changes every 10-12 weeks providing an endless choice throughout the year. Every Wednesday evening (January-November) a specially priced menu is on offer; 2 courses £16.95, 3 courses £19.95.

Opening times:
Tue-Thur 12.00 pm - 2.00 pm & 7.00 pm - 9.30 pm
Fri-Sat 12.00 pm - 2.00 pm & 6.00 pm - 9.30 pm

£5

The Plough Restaurant

Kimbolton Road
Bolnhurst
Bedfordshire
MK44 2EX
Tel: 01234 376274
Email: theplough@bolnhurst.com
www.bolnhurst.com

FOODIE
Reader Comment

"Excellent on all counts and the perfect place to escape the hustle and bustle at the weekend"
P. Edwards

This beautiful building traces its roots back to Tudor times. Its low beams, intriguing layout and few windows exert a huge influence on the character of the pub. Original features, candlelight and open fires create an intensely warm atmosphere whilst subtle lighting adds intimacy. It has that most sought-after, cocooning quality.

The kitchen is open to view from the bar and restaurant, a feature which draws you forward into the heart of the building. The sight and sound of a kitchen at work is irresistible, consumed by the delicious aromas after a few minutes inside the desire to eat is unbearable!

The service team provide the final touch. The noise and laughter ebbing through the building pays tribute to the relaxed and content atmosphere that they create. There is the most elusive balance between the formality that holds everything together and the informality that allows everyone to enjoy themselves.

The true joy of The Plough at Bolnhurst is the perfect trinity of atmosphere, service and sumptuous food.

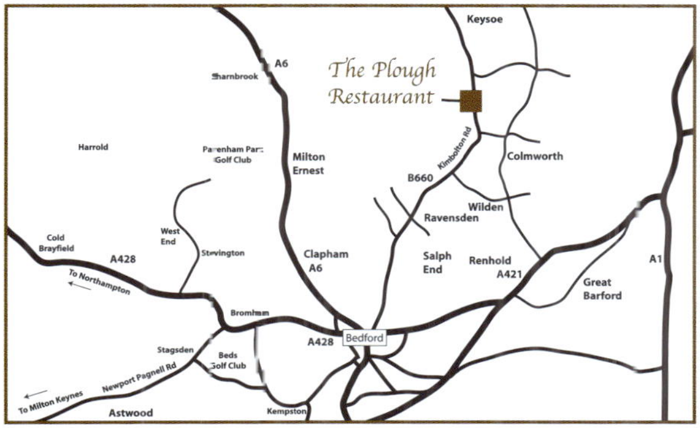

Food served times:
Tue-Sat 12.00 pm - 2.00 pm & 6.30 pm - 9.30 pm
Sun 12.00 pm - 2.00 pm

lunch dinner

Moreteyne Manor

Woburn Road
Marston Moreteyne
Bedfordshire
MK43 0NQ
Tel: 01234 767003
www.moreteynemanor.co.uk

FOODIE
Reader Comment

"Always a warm welcome and like the Tina Turner song - 'Simply the best, better than all the rest'"

Mr & Mrs S.E. Willis

Moreteyne Manor is a hidden treasure in the village of Marston Moreteyne, set amidst beautiful landscaped gardens surrounded by a moat this 16th Century country house is an exciting venue to discover. The Manor was acquired by chef Mark Hickman and his wife Jacqui in 1996 and over the years have built up a reputation of a warm, relaxing atmosphere and superb food.

The Manor offers a 30 cover restaurant and two function rooms. The Mulberry Room between 40 to 50 covers. The Betty Howe Suite a private dining room for 18 covers. Weddings are catered for from the romance of a few to the elegance of a marquee in the delightful gardens.

The à la carte menu is an exploration of the finest red and white meats, seafood and country fresh vegetables and an extensive wine list to complement. Quite simply, a journey into culinary perfection.

Opening times: Reservations only
Tuesday - Saturday

10%

Lunch Dinner

FT

ST. HELENA RESTAURANT

High Street
Elstow
Bedfordshire
MK42 9XP
Tel: 01234 344848

THE FOODIE AWARD 2008
Bedfordshire
winner
as voted by THE FOODIE Square Guide readers

FOODIE
Reader Comment

"This has to be one of the best restaurants in the country. I was very fortunate to be treated to a fantastic meal here"

J. Martin

With easy access from the A6 on the outskirts of Bedford is the small village of Elstow. In a secluded setting tucked behind a beautiful walled garden, you will find a 16th century private house which has been transformed to create St Helena Restaurant.

With style, elegance and a country home feeling of Englishness, it is home to a wonderful collection of antiques and fine paintings which makes it perfect to celebrate a special occasion, entertain important business clients or just an informal evening

Now in their 22nd year, brothers-in-law Raffaele and Franco offer an interesting and well prepared modern classic menu with Italian and French influence, accompanied by an excellent selection of fine and rare wines on a list of over 300 bins! In the winter the fires roar and in the summer a drink in the garden or near the pond precedes lunch or dinner perhaps in the elegant conservatory.

Fresh seafood including Cornish Lobster, Crab and Oysters from Colchester are available regularly as well as quality Scottish and English Lamb and Beef, Rare Breed Pork and local Game. Classic dishes with a twist can often be found on what is always a good choice menu.

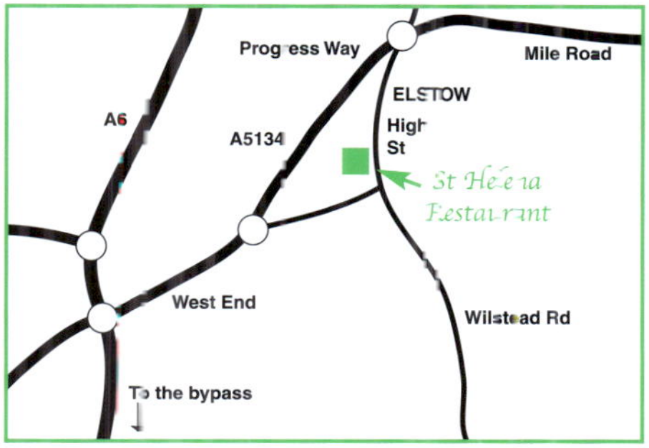

Opening times:
Tue-Fri 12.15 pm - 1.00 pm (last orders)
& 7.00 pm - 9.00 pm (last orders)
Sat 7.00 pm - 9.00 pm (last orders)

lunch dinner

Horse & Jockey

Church End
Ravensden
Bedfordshire
MK44 2RR
Tel: 01234 772319 **Fax:** 01234 772710
www.horseandjockey.info

FOODIE
Reader Comment

"Lovely food, friendly staff and a wonderfully relaxed atmosphere"

L. Fairweather

Only 5 minutes from Bedford yet in the heart of the countryside the Horse and Jockey at Church End, Ravensden is well worth a visit. Situated next to the beautiful old church of All Saints amidst thatched cottages it is an ideal place to unwind.

Recently taken over by Darron & Sarah Smith it has been completely restyled and now offers a wonderful atmosphere both as a pub and restaurant. Indoors or out there is the chance to relax. Whether you come just for a drink and one of Darron's locally famous snack pots or to dine in the restaurant you will not be disappointed.

This freehouse offers a range of beers and guest ales as well as an extensive wine list and a menu of freshly prepared high quality ever changing dishes. Chef Darron strongly believes in using the best quality ingredients with an emphasis on supporting local producers. The menu includes a great variety of game dishes when in season as well as a broad range of classics including Darron's signature dish of Belly Pork. In addition he also has an excellent fish menu that changes daily dependent on catch.

Darron and Sarah, with their welcoming staff, have created a venue with friendly atmosphere, excellent service and quality food at affordable prices.

Food served times:
Mon-Thur 12.00 pm - 2.30 pm & 6.00 pm - 9.00 pm
Fri-Sat 12.00 pm - 2.45 pm & 6.00 pm - 9.00 pm
Sun 12.00 pm - 3.00 pm & 6.00 pm - 8.00 pm

Paris House

Woburn Park, Woburn, Bedfordshire MK17 9QP
Tel: 01525 290692 **Fax:** 01525 290471
Email: info@parishouse.co.uk
www.parishouse.co.uk

FOODIE
Reader Comment

"Excellent veggie menu - best for miles! Beautiful setting and wonderful old fashioned service"
Mrs L. Cook

Situated in the most beautiful and idyllic surroundings of Woburn Deer Park you will find one of England's finest restaurants 'Paris House'. Originally built in 1878 for the Paris Exhibition, Paris House was dismantled and rebuilt, piece by piece on the Woburn Estate.

Chef/Proprietor, Peter Chandler is celebrating 25 years since opening Paris House, following 14 years training with The Roux Brothers. The menu at Paris House combines the best of classic French cuisine with a contemporary and innovative culinary style at tremendous value for money. A full vegetarian menu is available and we also cater for children. A 3 course weekday luncheon is just £25.00 per head and a 3 course dinner is £60.00 per head. Every Tuesday night there is a 3 course set dinner with a vegetarian option for £25.00 per head. The wines are selected from an extensive list ranging from the house wine, modestly priced at £19.50 per bottle to the most distinguished, from the New World and Old.

The unique surroundings are picturesque and tranquil, with a warm, welcoming and friendly atmosphere. In the Summer, relax with pre dinner drinks on the terrace overlooking the Deer Park, or in the cooler months in the warm, cosy Bar. Paris House seats a maximum of 45 people in the main dining room with a private dining room seating up to 16 people. Perfect for any occasion.

THE FOODIE AWARD 2007 Bedfordshire

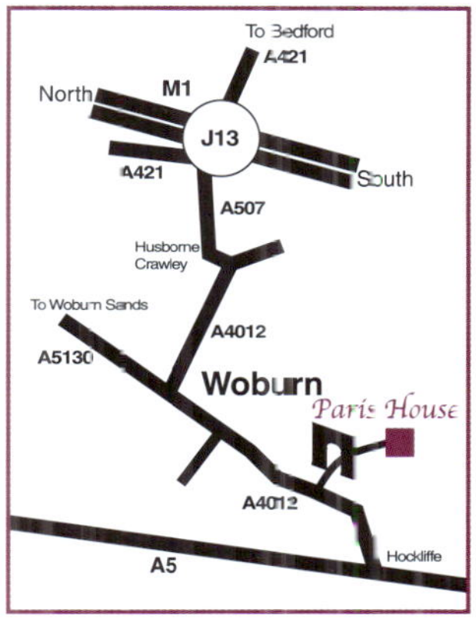

Opening times:
Tue-Sat for Lunch 12.00 noon (last orders 1.45 pm) & Dinner 7.00 pm (last orders 9.30 pm)
Sun for Lunch only 12.00 noon (last orders 1.45 pm)
Pre-ordering for a quick lunch is available on request.
Weddings, private parties & corporate functions catered for.

Lunch Dinner

The Park

98 Kimbolton Road
Bedford
MK40 2PA
Tel: 01234 409305
Fax: 01234 365754
Email: info@theparkbedford.co.uk
www.theparkbedford.co.uk

FOODIE
Reader Comment

"I love the relaxed atmosphere and unstuffy food"

A. Westfield

The Park is quite simply striking, modern furnishings melt into the natural surfaces brought to life using imaginative lighting. From the conservatory restaurant, comfy bar to the covered/heated courtyard you are assured of a very warm welcome from attentive unfussy staff.

The main menu has a wide range of dishes to delight every taste. Salads and stone-fired pizzas vie with steak and other traditional favourites prepared in the unique TPI way, such as duck breast with spinach and potato rosti, smothered in a vodka and black cherry sauce. At lunchtimes they also serve a variety of nibbles, grazing boards for deli lovers, and speciality sandwiches with unusual tasty fillings.

They source and use the freshest ingredients possible and supporting the local community is extremely important to The Park. On Thursday evenings they provide fayre from within Bedfordshire. Everything on the specials menu is grown and reared within the Bedfordshire boundaries. Dine in the knowledge that you are eating local and reducing your carbon footprint.

Food served times:
Mon-Sat 12.00 pm - 3.00 pm & 5.30 pm - 9.00 pm
Sun 12.00 pm - 6.00 pm
Bookings advisable

£5

FT O

Menzies Flitwick Manor

Flitwick Manor
Church Road
Flitwick
Bedfordshire MK45 1AE
Tel: 01525 712242
Fax: 01525 718753
Email: flitwick@menzieshotels.co.uk
www.bookmenzies.com

FOODIE
Reader Comment

"We had an absolutely top class meal here and in such a grand setting too"

W. Atkins

Situated just two miles from junction 12 of the M1 and only 40 minutes by train from London's Kings Cross, Menzies Flitwick Manor sits within it's own tranquil gardens and wooded parklands. And is the perfect setting for a business breakfast, an informal lunch with friends, traditional afternoon tea in the gardens or a special dinner.

Acknowledged as one of the top 200 hotels in the country by the AA and award winning restaurant for fine dining. The restaurant offers the ultimate, affordable dining experience which for all its grandeur and style is both relaxing and comfortable. Enjoy drinks on the terrace overlooking the croquet lawns, a candlelit dinner followed by coffee and handmade petit fours in the elegantly restored Music Room. Service is unobtrusive, friendly and accommodating.

There are two private rooms fully equipped for conferences and meetings as well as for formal dinners and celebrations The Chef and his experienced brigade use the freshest seasonal produce sourced locally whenever possible to create imaginative dishes capturing natural flavours.

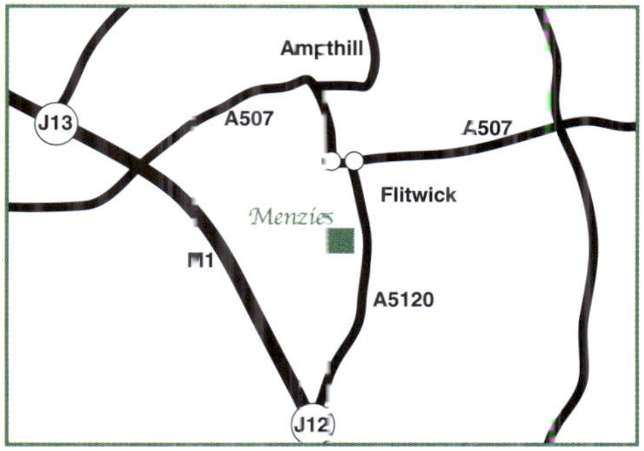

Food Served times:
Every day
12.00 pm - 2.30 pm
7.00 pm - 9.30 pm

£5 10%

Lunch Dinner

The Kings Head

Ivinghoe
Leighton Buzzard
Bedfordshire
LU7 9EB
Tel: 01296 668388
Fax: 01296 668107
Email: info@kingsheadivinghoe.co.uk
www.kingsheadivinghoe.co.uk

FOODIE
Reader Comment

"We had a delicious meal, the wine list was extensive and all served in a very pleasant manner"

Mrs Clarke

The Kings Head is situated in the very heart of the picturesque village of Ivinghoe, on the Beds, Bucks and Herts borders. This ivy covered building dates back to times when quality and service went hand in hand and happily it still exists here to this day.

We pride ourselves on good old fashioned service and serious professionalism. Georges de Maison's passion for quality food, meticulous attention to detail and impeccable service ensures that your dining experience will be memorable if not unique. Soft candlelight and shimmering silverware complement the restaurants already inviting ambience.

Chef de Cuisine Jonathan O'Keeffe is famed for his skillfully prepared eclectic menus. Only the very best and freshest of produce is used with much of this sourced locally. After lunch or perhaps before dinner, why not take a stroll around the village and visit the windmill. If the weather is inclement take the opportunity sit back in one of our comfy chairs, order your favourite aperitif and let the world go by! Alternatively, take a few moments to explore over 50 original works of art which adorn the walls.

A banqueting suite is available for private dining up to 40 guests. For small conferences, weddings and larger functions marquees can be put in the garden.

We promise a warm welcome and look forward to seeing you soon.

Food served times:
Mon-Sat 12.00 pm - last orders 2.00 pm
& 7.00 pm - last orders 9.15 pm
Sun 12.00 pm - last orders 2.00 pm

lunch dinner

The Prince of Wales

24 Bedford Street
Ampthill
Bedfordshire
MK45 2NB
Tel: 01525 840504
Fax: 01525 840574
Email: ricksbar1@aol.com
www.princeofwales-ampthill.com

FOODIE
Reader Comment

"Lovely food, staff very friendly - will definitely go again!"
L. Keens

Welcome to the newly refurbished Prince of Wales, where superb accommodation, memorable food and quality liquor meets informality and a relaxing atmosphere in a unique but comfortable setting. The Prince of Wales is a traditional red brick town inn, where the emphasis is on hospitality - from the welcoming ambience and the attentive service to the quality of the eating experience. Lovingly refurbished, The Prince of Wales delights with its individually designed surroundings and consideration to detail.

Fresh flowers, new oak and flagstone flooring throughout combine to make the perfect setting to relax over coffee or drinks, have lunch or dinner, or enjoy al fresco dining in the garden. Recently renovated and refurbished, the 5 individually designed en-suite bedrooms provide a welcoming retreat making for an even more enjoyable stay!

The Prince of Wales now boasts a delightful restaurant, a first class chef, a unique wine list and a sophisticated bar offering stylish fine dining and bar food alongside exciting drinks and cocktails. Using only fresh produce which is locally sourced and freshly prepared on the premises by Jaeson the "larger than life" chef. Traditional Sunday roast, 2 courses; £14, 3 courses; £16. Monday night features "Taste of England", 2 courses; £15, 3 courses; £20. Whether it's a meal for two or a group dinner, the Prince of Wales is a welcoming place to dine.

The Prince of Wales has the perfect atmosphere for every social occasion. Private parties of up to 100 people are catered for. the restaurant is ideal for wedding receptions, banquets, parties or any special occasion. Alternatively, they also offer outside catering.

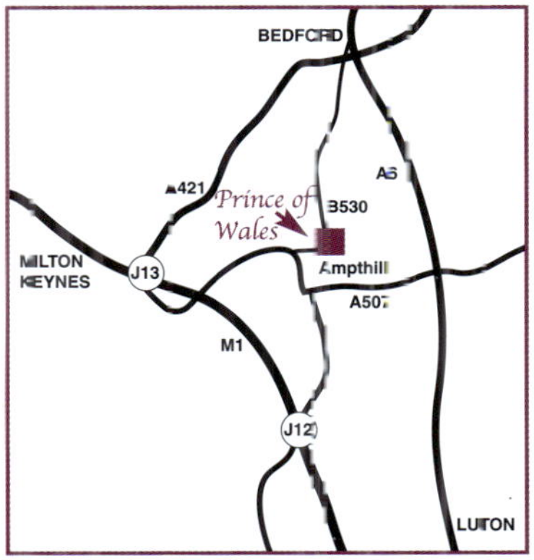

Opening times:
Mon-Sat 11.00 am - 11.00 pm
Sun 12 noon - 4.00 pm

Vouchers valid Monday to Friday only
£5 10%

FT O B

The White Hart

Brook Lane
Flitton
Bedfordshire
MK45 5EJ
Tel: 01525 862022
Email: philhale@btconnect.com
www.whitehartflitton.co.uk

FOODIE
Reader Comment

"A beautiful setting, very tasty menu and excellent service"
J. Matthews

Building on the success at The Chester Arms in Chicheley, Phil and Clare Hale have moved their award winning experience to "The White Hart at Flitton".

Open for lunch and dinner Tuesday to Saturday and a traditional roast lunch on Sunday, the highly experienced team in the kitchen, lead by award winning chef Steve Mascall, offer fresh food, freshly prepared with the emphasis on doing things simply but more importantly; properly. A selection of snacks for that light meal at lunchtime, or for something a little more substantial, daily delivered fresh fish or as a member of the Scotch Beef Club, the opportunity to tackle one of our Aberdeen Angus steaks cut to the size of your choice.

With everything you would expect from a village pub, there is something for everyone, from well kept real ales to a wide range of quality, personally tasted wines, all available by the glass and a large selection of soft drinks, teas and coffees.

Set in beautifully kept large grounds in the tranquil village of Flitton, close to Flitwick and Ampthill, The White Hart offers a 'picture postcard' setting overlooking Flitton Moor and St John the Baptist Church. With grounds and facilities for marquees and outside entertainment, The White Hart is the perfect location to celebrate birthdays, anniversaries, christenings and weddings.

Come and join us for lunch or dinner, a warm welcome awaits you!

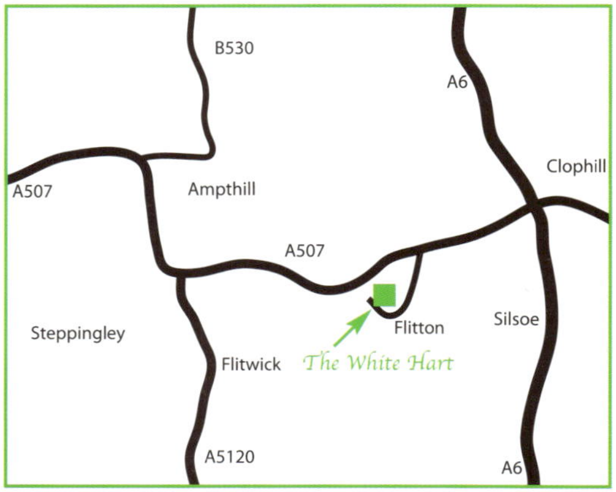

Food served times:
Tue-Thur 12.00 pm - 2.00 pm & 7.00 pm - 9.00 pm
Fri-Sat 12.00 pm- 2.00 pm & 6.30 pm - 9.30 pm
Sun 12.00 pm- 3.00 pm

Galloway's

Aberdeen House
22-23 Market Place
Woburn
Bedfordshire
MK17 9PZ
Tel: 01525 290496
www.gallowayswoburn.com

FOODIE
Reader Comment

"Delicious menu and attentive service with a lively atmosphere"

J. Edwards

'Party bookings and pre-booked lunches are welcomed'

Galloway's is a family run restaurant providing a relaxed informal atmosphere in a Grade II listed building in the heart of the historic village of Woburn.

Tuesday is our Pasta, Steak and Fish evening and Wednesday to Saturday we offer an à la carte menu which changes regularly, using only the best fresh produce. On Sunday we add our traditional roast selection to the menu for both lunchtime and evening service and we always have delicious vegetarian dishes. We are now open Friday lunchtimes too.

We will be celebrating our 13th Anniversary in November.

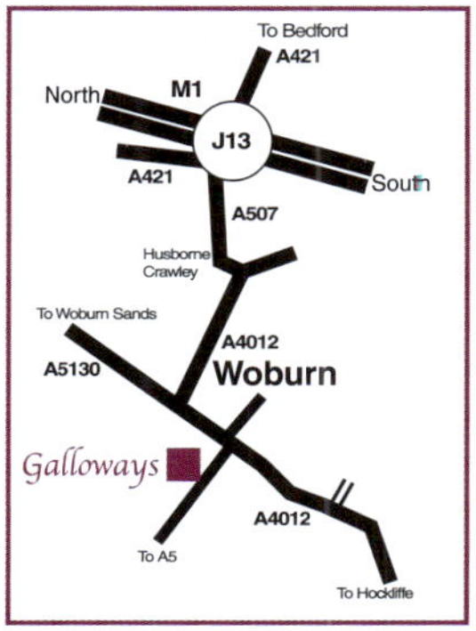

Opening times:
Tue-Thur 7.00 pm - 10.00 pm
Fri 12 noon - 2.00 pm & 7.00 pm - 10.00 pm
Sat 7.00 pm - 10.00 pm
Sun 12 noon - 2.00 pm & 7.00 pm - 9.30 pm

£5

FT O

The Green Man

Church End
Eversholt
Milton Keynes
MK17 9DU
Tel: 01525 288111
Email: info@greenmaneversholt.com
www.greenmaneversholt.com

FOODIE
Reader Comment
"A really friendly welcome and gorgeous food in a splendid country setting" T. Sherman

Located in the picturesque village of Eversholt, 2 minutes from Woburn, is the traditional Green Man Pub and Restaurant. Overlooking the church and cricket ground at the front and boasting a lovely patio garden at the back, it is a perfect location for a drink or a meal. In June 2008, The Green Man became a Freehouse; now owned and run by London trained husband and wife team. Refurbishment has already started on the garden area and the inside of the building will be changed in October 2008 bringing a real country pub back to life.

The menu offers a range of dishes to cater for all tastes. Choose from the quick lunch of classic baguettes and jacket potatoes or pub favourites of Grain Mustard and Honey Roast Ham with Free Range Eggs and Cumberland Sausage Toad in the Hole. For a more discerning taste, they specialise in fresh fish and a specials board that changes daily. For the drinkers, The Green Man serves real ales that change on a regular basis and a large selection of wines by the glass. The chef does all possible to ensure that the ingredients are either sourced locally or certainly from Britain and all dishes are created and cooked on the premises. The Green Man offers Pig and Lamb Roasts either at the pub or at your preferred location for any special events.

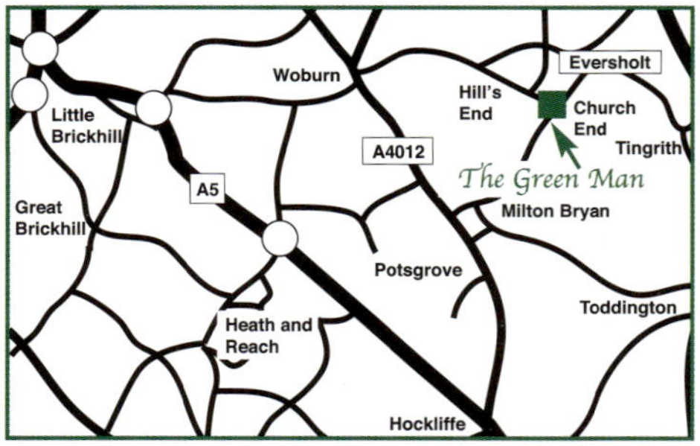

Food served times:
Tue-Sat 12.00 pm - 2.30 pm & 7.00 pm - 9.00 pm
Sun 12.00 pm - 3.00 pm
Bar opening times:
Mon 5.00 pm - close
Tue-Fri 12.00 pm - 2.30 pm & 5.00 pm - close
Sat 12.00 pm - close
Sun 12.00 pm - 6.00 pm

£5 10%
Vouchers valid Mon-Thurs only

The Boot at Sarratt

The Green, Sarratt, Rickmansworth, Hertfordshire WD3 6BL
Tel: 01923 262247
Email: info@thebootsarratt.co.uk **www.thebootsarratt.co.uk**

FOODIE
Reader Comment

"The perfect country pub with great food"

B. Pearce

This quintessential Grade II, 18th century freehouse inn is situated in an idyllic setting, opposite the village green in Sarratt. Although set in peaceful surroundings, it is only 3 miles from junction 18 of the M25, so easily accessible.

Built in 1739, The Boot still retains many original, character features. With a warm and inviting ambience, exposed beams and brick built open fireplaces, The Boot offers a 'home from home' welcome with its traditional public bar area, large beer garden, children's play area, 22 seater restaurant and patio. Well behaved children, dogs and horses are all very welcome - although we do expect you to leave your horse outside!

Our food offering ranges from traditional home cooked bar meals and snacks to delicious à la carte options. We also offer an innovative dining experience with our Black Rock Grill; food is brought to your table, sizzling on a volcanic rock heated to 440 degrees celsius. It's fun, it's sociable and it's also a healthier option as no oil or fats are used.

We stock a large selection of good quality wines from all over the world as well as an excellent selection of real ales, some of which are sourced from a local brewery.

From romantic dinners for two, wedding celebrations, corporate functions, private parties or just a quick pint to unwind, The Boot is the perfect place to enjoy any occasion!

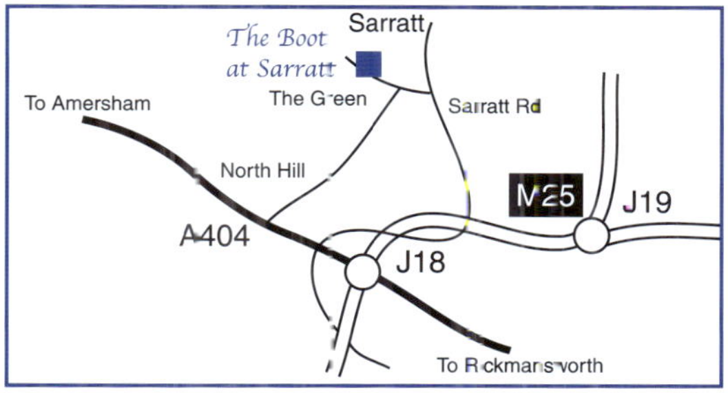

Opening times:	Food served times:
Mon-Fri 11.00 am - 3.00 pm	**Mon-Fri** 12.00 pm - 2.30 pm
& 5.30 pm - 11.00 pm	**Tue-Thur** 6.30 pm - 9.00 pm
Sat 11.00 am - 11.00 pm	**Fri** 6.30 pm - 10.30 pm
Sun 12.00 pm - 10.30 pm	**Sat** 12.00 pm - 10.30 pm
	Sun 12.00 pm - 8.00 pm

The Silver Cup

St Albans Road
Harpenden
Hertfordshire
AL5 2JF
Tel: 01582 713095
Email: info@silvercup.co.uk
www.silvercup.co.uk

FOODIE
Reader Comment

"Excellent, well cooked original cuisine and friendly service"

L. Moss

Sitting on the idyllic Harpenden Common the Silver Cup lies between St. Albans and Luton and can be easily reached from the M1, M25, A5 and Luton Airport.

We are a family run, traditional coaching inn that fuses the past and the future of hospitality. "The Silver Cup way" is a philosophy that runs through everything that we do. Our friendly, well trained staff are part of the family and they all play their part in creating a clean, relaxed and friendly environment for you to unwind, whatever the reason for your visit.

Whether you dine from our AA Rossette winning à la carte menu, our pub menu with a range of classic pub fayre or you opt for our exceptionally good value lunch set menu, you can be assured of the quality of the ingredients along with the care and attention taken preparing them.

We know that the key to a good pub is the beer so we employ the same hygiene principles in our cellar as we do in our kitchen. By nurturing all our beer from delivery until it is ready to be served we can be sure the lager is cold, lively and crisp while the Cask Marque standard ale is clear, frothy and full of flavour.

We are lucky to have a good following of regulars in the bar, restaurant and our AA Four Star B&B but we are always on the look out for more! Liz, Michael, Jon and all the staff look forward to seeing you soon...

Opening times:
Mon-Sat 7.30 am - 11.00 pm
Sun 8.30 am - 10.30 pm

lunch dinner

Just 32

32 Sun Street, Hitchin, Herts SG5 1AH
Tel: 01462 455666
Email: david@just32.com
www.just32.com

THE FOODIE AWARD 2008 Hertfordshire winner
as voted by THE FOODIE Square Guide readers

FOODIE *Reader Comment*

"Consistent quality, great service, innovative menu, quality wine list - love it!"

M. Beswick

Excellent write-ups in the Hertfordshire magazine and a very good review in the Sunday Times after a visit from Mr Michael Winner in 2006.

Since opening in February 1999, Just 32 has built a reputation for many reasons; the excellent freshly cooked food, the friendly staff, the ambience and above all a feeling you are eating somewhere very special.

Housed in a building over 400 years old, Just 32 is situated just off the market square in the centre of this historic town. The décor includes exposed beams, subtle lighting, table linen and fresh flowers. This all helps to promote a comfortable, peaceful atmosphere where the service is a joy and you will feel relaxed and never rushed. The setting is perfect for all occasions including family celebrations, business meetings, romantic dinners, small weddings or just a meal with good friends.

We offer a full à la carte menu, including vegetarian dishes, a separate lunch menu and also a mid-week specials menu where you can enjoy either a 2 or 3 course meal (lunch and dinner) from only £14.95. Our à la carte menu changes every month and our lunch menu more frequently.

We look forward to welcoming you to our restaurant soon.

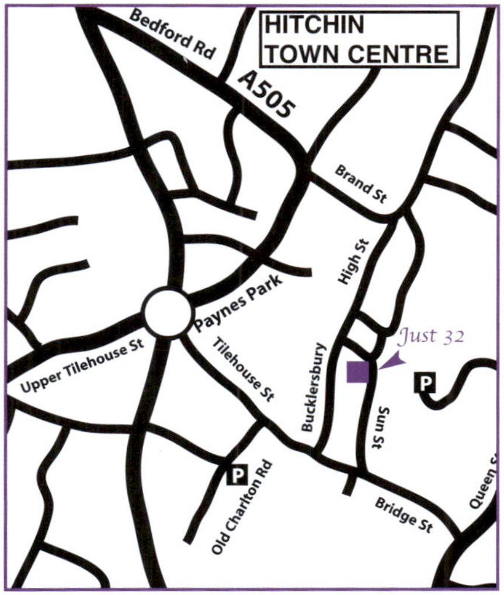

Mille Feuille of Summer Berries with Lemon Cream

Slow Roasted Belly Pork in a Honey & White Wine Sauce

Food served times:
Tue-Thur 12.00 pm - 2.30 pm & 6.30 pm - 9.30 pm
Fri-Sat 12.00 pm - 2.30 pm & 6.30 pm - 10.00 pm

Lunch Dinner
A C

10%
Voucher valid Tues to Thurs off à la carte menu only

The Restaurant at Tewin Bury Farm

B1000 Hertford Road
Nr Welwyn
Herts AL6 0JB
Tel: 01438 841490
Fax: 01438 840440
Email: restaurant@tewinbury.co.uk
www.tewinbury.co.uk

FOODIE
Reader Comment

"Amazing food and perfect service - it doesn't get much better than this"

P. Winter

Set in the beautiful Hertfordshire countryside along the river Mimram, The Tewin Bury Restaurant can be found on the outskirts of the village of Tewin (which lies between Welwyn Garden City and Hertford).

Our restaurant has enjoyed an excellent reputation for its food and service for more than 20 years and recently received a well deserved refurbishment. Solid oak tables and chairs, complemented by new crockery and glassware have given our restaurant a fantastic contemporary look, whilst still in keeping with our country setting.

Our dedicated kitchen brigade, lead by Mennel Welch our Head Chef (read more about him in the chef's profile section), create imaginative and seasonal menus and aim to use mainly local ingredients.

At lunchtime we offer our à la carte menu, complemented by our daily specials on the Black Boards and to enable us to satisfy our corporate client's needs for a quick lunch we have recently introduced our Business Lunch Menu.

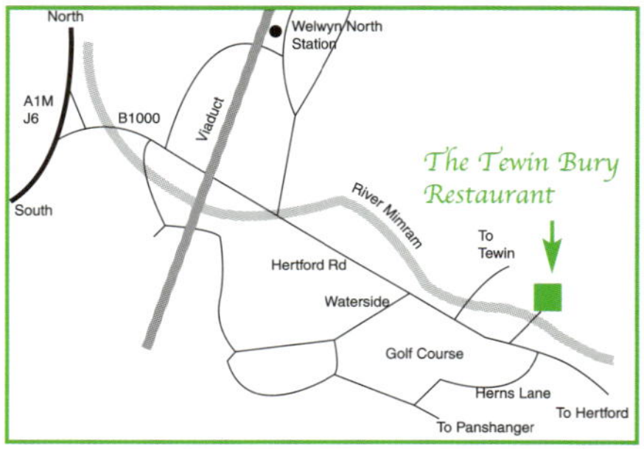

For dinner, you can choose between our à la carte menu or our weekly changing table d'hote menu. Throughout the day we are also open for breakfast, morning coffee, small snacks and afternoon tea.

From early Spring until late Autumn you can enjoy all of these alfresco on our lovely terrace complemented with large umbrellas and heaters.

It is the perfect scene for an unpretentious meal and offers a warm atmosphere for all special occasions or family get-togethers.

The Foodie Award 2007 Hertfordshire

Food served times:
Mon-Sat 12.00 pm - 2.00 pm & 6.30 - 9.30 pm
Sun 12.00 pm- 2.30 pm, & 3.30 pm - 8.00 pm

£5

The Bricklayers Arms

Hog Pits Bottom, Flaunden, Hemel Hempstead HP3 0PH
Tel: 01442 833322 **Email:** goodfood@bricklayersarms.com
www.bricklayersarms.com

FOODIE *Reader Comment*

"A cut above the rest - for fab food and great service"

J. Rolls

"Hertfordshire's Dining Pub of The Year" – The Good Pub Guide 2008
Michelin Guide Recommendation 2008/9
"Commendation Award 2008" – Harden's Guide
Claude Paillet "Chef of the Year Award" – The Publican
"Freehouse of The Year Award" – The Publican
"Restaurant of the Year 2006" – The Foodie Square Guide

The Bricklayers Arms is tucked away in the tiny Hertfordshire village of Flaunden which you can find at the end of the winding lanes which snake between Chipperfield and Latimer. A picturesque pub in a beautiful location often featured in film and tv series.

Alvin and Sally Michaels recently refurbished this ivy clad 18th Century listed building. You are sure to receive a warm welcome and enjoy the atmosphere with its low wooden beams and real log fire. Over the past three years, The Bricklayers Arms has certainly gained an excellent reputation for its English traditional and French Fusion menu created by its French chefs. You can enjoy the same menu throughout the restaurant and pub seven days a week with dishes ranging at lunchtime from their famous Steak and Kidney Guinness Pie to matured Fillet Steaks and local game. The evening menu offers several starters including, Pan Fried Foie Gras to Brochette of Pan Fried Tiger Prawns on a Rosemary Stick served with a Seasonal Vegetable Stir-fry and a Light Curry Cream to main courses of Best End of Lamb served with a Pea Flan and Chicken Mozzarella with a Smoked Bacon and Mushroom Sauce.

The Bricklayers Arms is now well known for their own home smoked fish and meats; starters include a selection of fish served with a Coriander Butter and their Home Made Sweet Onion Jam or Home Smoked Duck with Foie Gras Shavings with a Honey Dressed Salad in Filo Basket. You'll always find a selection of fresh fish dishes and vegetarian options on the menu. Every day the Bricklayers Arms offer tantalising specials of the day.

THE FOODIE AWARD 2006 Hertfordshire

Food served times:
Mon-Sat 12.00 pm - 2.30 pm & 6.30 pm - 9.30 pm
Sun 12.00 pm - 3.30 pm & 6.30 pm - 8.30 pm

£5

FT O

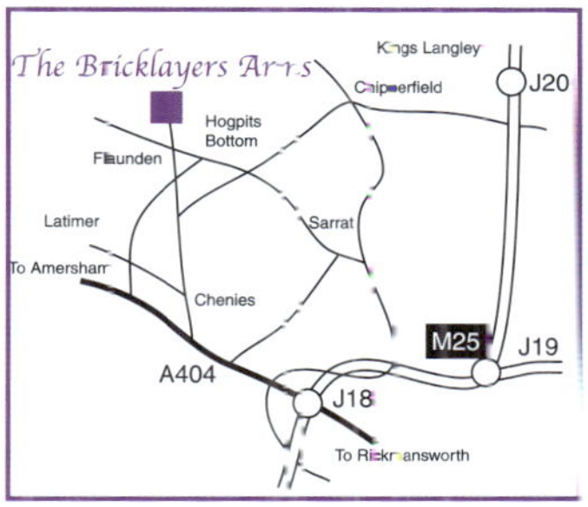

The Cabinet AT REED

High Street, Reed, Royston, Hertfordshire SG8 8AH
Tel: 01763 848366
Email: thecabinet@btconnect.com
www.thecabinetatreed.co.uk

FOODIE
Reader Comment

"A charming place to visit with the added benefit of extremely good food and wine"

J. Mullucks

The Cabinet in Reed is back at its best.

A beautifully preserved 16th Century Inn and restaurant with low beamed ceilings, a cosy fireplace, serene country setting and a welcoming pint of real ale; The Cabinet is a place most people think only exists in novels.

Angus Martin (formally executive chef at Fortnum and Mason) is driving the kitchen and provenance of the food; locally sourced if possible. Tracey Hale, former Cambridge restaurateur, keeps a keen eye on service and all wine matters (supplied by friend and fellow foodie Paul Bowes of "Bacchanalia").

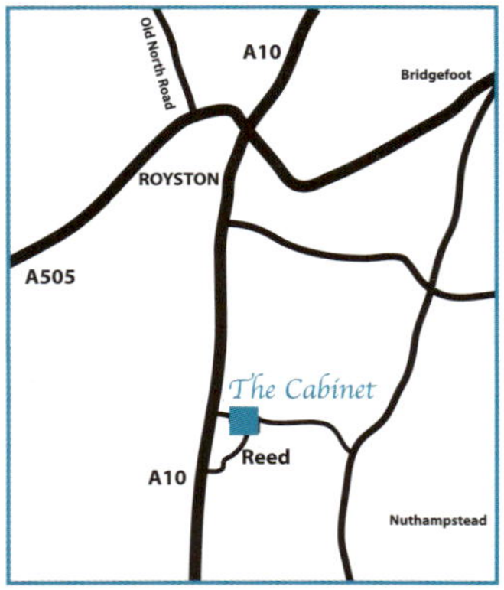

The menu changes monthly to take advantage of the best produce available. On offer is an award winning mix of menus from an easy and relaxed supper menu to the fast and punchy Snug and Bar menu featuring all your favorite pub meals, also Sunday lunch for those in search of a traditional roast with a pint of Real Ale, and if the great British weather allows; a fantastic alfresco terrace.

Situated in the small village of Reed, a couple of miles away from the market town of Buntingford and near Royston, you will find The Cabinet just off the A10 London to Cambridge road within easy travelling distance from London.

Food served times:
Tue-Sat 12.00 pm - 3.00 pm & 6.00 pm - 9.00 pm
Sun 12.00 pm - 3.00 pm
Bar opening times:
Mon 6.00 pm - 11.00 pm
Tue-Fri 12.00 pm - 3.00 pm & 6.00 pm - 11.00 pm
Sat-Sun All day
Bank Holiday open for food & drink from 12.00 pm

10%

FT O

The Fox & Hounds

2 High Street
Hunsdon
Ware
Hertfordshire
SG12 8NH
Tel: 01279 843999
Fax: 01279 841092
Email: info@foxandhounds-hunsdon.co.uk
www.foxandhounds-hunsdon.co.uk

FOODIE *Reader Comment*

"A wonderful place to savour exceptionally good food in a beautiful village setting"

A. Chambers

The Fox & Hounds is a family run establishment in the pretty village of Hunsdon Now in its third year, it is established as one of Hertfordshire's leading gastro pubs, receiving impressive reviews and accolades in numerous press articles and guides. Chef/proprietor James Rix has previously worked in some of London's most celebrated eateries.

Everything is made in-house and the menu changes daily making the best of good quality seasonal produce. Rare breed meats and locally shot game feature and shellfish is delivered daily from the East and South coasts. Sample dishes include Rabbit Livers, Asparagus & Soft Boiled Egg, Terrine Chutney and Toast and Smoked Eel, Potato Pancake, Beetroot and Horseradish. For main course why not try the popular Cote de Boeuf, Sauce Béarnaise and Hand Cut Chips or 'Label Anglais' Chicken, Peas, Morels and Broad Beans Finish off with Bitter Chocolate Tart and Espresso Ice Cream. There is an interesting wine list with a good selection offered by the glass or carafe.

The pub has a friendly, informal atmosphere with a comfy laid back bar, log fire, leather sofas and local ales. The homely dining room features a chandelier and is popular for gatherings of families and friends and for private functions.

The large garden comes into its own in the summer with a large covered/heated patio and children's play area - great to keep the children entertained whilst having a quiet drink or bite to eat.

Opening times:
Tue - Sat 12 noon - 3.00 pm & 6.30 pm - 10.00 pm
Sun 12 noon - 3.00 pm

Zodiac Restaurant

Hanbury Manor Hotel
Ware
Hertfordshire SG12 0SD
Tel: 01920 487722
Fax: 01920 487692
www.hanbury-manor.com

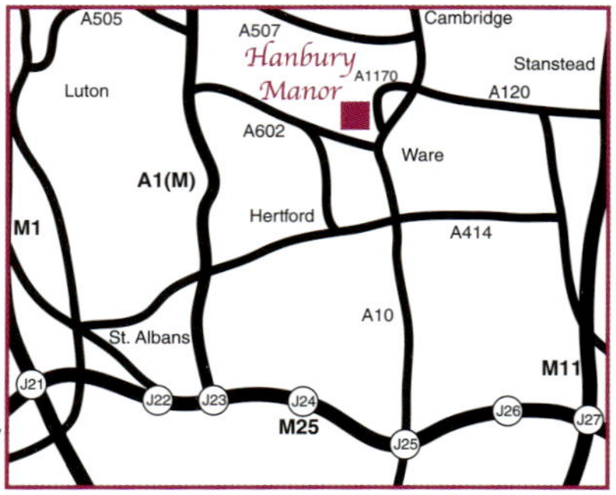

The award winning Zodiac Restaurant at Hanbury Manor is set amid 200 acres of glorious countryside, with stunning views and magnificent interior, providing the perfect backdrop for a truly gastronomic experience. From the imaginative menu, using the freshest and best quality ingredients to the extensive wine list, The Zodiac Restaurant is a must for all food lovers.

Make the most of the summer and dine on the newly opened Zodiac terrace or for those of you who wish to see the chef in action a chef's table for up to six people is available, serving the seven course 'Taste of Hanbury' menu. After your meal, relax with a coffee or fine cognac in the wood-panelled Oak Hall or take a stroll in the grounds.

Opening times: **Mon** closed
Tue-Fri 12.30 pm - 2.00 pm & 7.00 pm - 9.30 pm
Sat 7.00 pm - 9.45 pm
Sun 12.30 pm - 2.00 pm

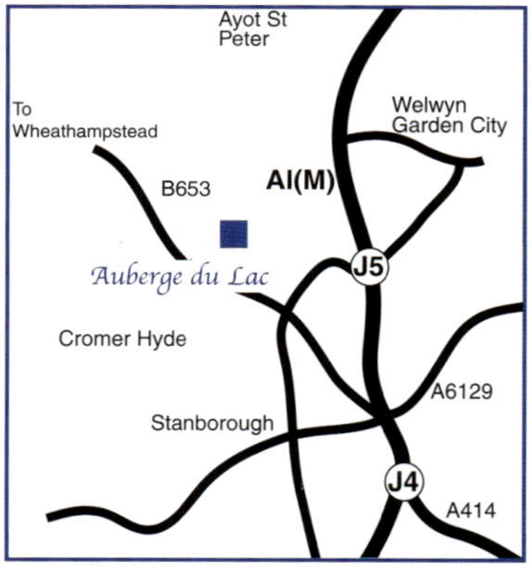

Auberge du Lac

Brocket Hall
Welwyn
Hertfordshire AL8 7XG
Tel: 01707 368888
Fax: 01707 368898
Email: auberge@brocket-hall.co.uk
www.brocket-hall.co.uk

Auberge du Lac is the inspired result of a comprehensive and elegant design and refurbishment programme. Set in the magnificent parkland of Brocket Hall, Auberge du Lac promises to uphold the finest culinary standards and will further enhance Brocket Hall's reputation for excellence.

A former Hunting Lodge dating back to 1760, the building sits proudly alongside the water's edge in its own peaceful environment, overlooking the splendour of the Estate.

Opening times: Lunch **Tue-Sun** 12.00 - 2.30 pm
Dinner **Tue-Sat** 7.00 - 10.00 pm

Exquisitely furnished, with panoramic views beyond its own garden setting on the Broadwater.

Auberge du Lac provides a culinary delight in this most beautiful setting, yet only 40 minutes from central London.

The Wollaston Inn

87 London Road
Wollaston
Northants
NN29 7QS
Tel: 01933 663161
Email: info@wollaston-inn.co.uk
www.wollaston-inn.co.uk

"Wonderful food, great atmosphere and service - this place has it all"

R. Hurst

FOODIE
Reader Comment

Situated in the Village of Wollaston on the borders of Northamptonshire, Bedfordshire and Buckinghamshire the 350 year old Wollaston Inn has been revitalised in the past 5 years by Chef/Patron Chris Spencer.

With a passion for seafood and inspired by fresh, seasonal, regional food the restaurant offers a variety of food throughout the day. Both the evening à la carte and lunch menus offer the best of traditional British dishes alongside some classic Mediterranean and internationally influenced choices. Running alongside these is the daily changing fresh seafood menu using produce delivered daily from fish markets around Britain. On Sundays there is a traditional Sunday roast lunch and, like every other day food is served at all times throughout the day.

There are plenty of choices of places to eat - there is a main restaurant with an open fire roaring through the winter, in the summer you can walk out through the french doors and sit out on the sun drenched patio, the bar is available for a casual lunch or just enjoy a coffee relaxing on the Italian leather sofas. There are also two additional rooms that are ideal for family gatherings, business meetings or small social events.

As well as the two private dining rooms there is the spacious function room available for weddings, celebrations and business meetings. With 20 years of experience within the industry Chris can offer you bespoke menus and a personal service that few other venues can match.

Food served:
Mon-Sat 11.00 am - 10.00 pm
Sun 12.00 pm - 10.00 pm

£5 10%

The Vine House Hotel & Restaurant

100 High Street, Paulerspury,
Northamptonshire NN12 7NA
Tel: 01327 811267 **Fax:** 01327 811309
Email: info@vinehousehotel.com
www.vinehousehotel.com

FOODIE
Reader Comment

"Absolutely superb in all respects and I eagerly look forward to my next visit"
T. Soames

Proprietors, chef and host Marcus & Julie Springett are devoted to their 300 year old Northamptonshire stone Vine House Hotel & Restaurant in Paulerspury and have attained a multi award winning reputation for offering outstanding cuisine and a warm personal welcome for all their guests.

The restaurant is open year round attracting diners both local and from far and wide on a satisfied quest for the best outside of London, providing a fusion of traditional English and modern continental cuisine with a twist.

Located on the doorstep of Silverstone Race Circuit and Towcester for Horseracing it is handy for sporting fixtures thus frequented by participants and enthusiasts as well as visitors on shopping sprees to nearby Milton Keynes or Bicester Village. Others come for a stop-over change of scene, or celebration without the drive home. This top notch restaurant with individual rooms, named after famous wine making grapes and bedecked with antiques plus every modern facility, sets The Vine House apart from any hostelry in the region.

Choose alfresco summer eating in the unique Garden Folly or cosy fireside cream teas in the aqua lounge bar, or lunch or dinner in the 33 cover dining room from a daily changed menu that never fails to delight even the most regular visitor. Out of this world chocolates round off a meal, devotedly made on the premises by Chef Marcus as well as ice creams and breads. Indeed all dishes are from locally sourced ingredients, rare breed meats and interesting marriages of flavours that excite the taste buds.

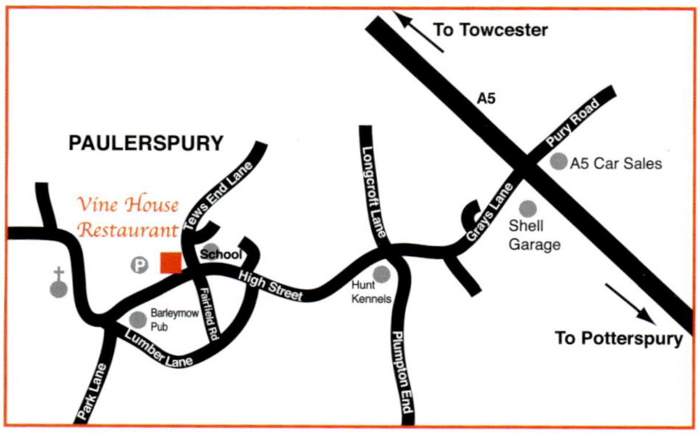

Food Served times:
Lunch **Tue-Sat** 12.30 pm - 1.45 pm
Dinner **Mon-Sun** 6.30 pm - 10.00 pm
Special openings on Sunday for events and stopovers / residents

£5

Murrays

Whittlebury Hall Hotel & Spa
Whittlebury
Nr Towcester
Northants
NN12 8QH
Tel: 01327 857857
Fax: 01327 857867
Email: reservations@whittleburyhall.co.uk
www.whittleburyhall.co.uk

AA Two AA rosettes for fine food

enjoyEngland.com ★★★★ HOTEL

enjoyEngland.com Silver AWARD

THE FOODIE AWARD 2008 Northamptonshire winner as voted by THE FOODIE Square Guide readers

When you have a passion for food...
Murrays is a must, boasting 2 AA Rosettes for its fine cuisine.

Murrays provides a relaxing venue to enjoy the creative dishes presented by our award winning Chef and his brigade.

Lifestyles today show an ever increasing interest in food as a fashion and Murrays menu, which changes regularly, provides our guests with the opportunity to taste the latest blends of flavours and ingredients to make your visit to Murrays truly memorable.

Fillet of Aged Casterbridge Beef

Lemon & Raspberry Mille Feuille

Our philosophy is quite simple; cook the finest carefully sourced ingredients and simply add our own twists and innovation. Our style could be described as modern British with influences from international and classical based cookery. All food, from the appetisers to the desserts are produced in-house from carefully created recipes, no dish is left to chance.

Whilst relaxing in the lounge and during dinner you can reminisce on the F1 commentary years of Murray Walker as we display a collection of photographs with F1 celebrities and also display some unique anecdotes of his memorable career.

Throughout the year Murrays hosts a variety of gourmet dining events, for more details go to www.whittleburyhall.co.uk or to book a table call 0845 400 0001.

Please bear in mind this is a dining experience not a quick bite in the local!

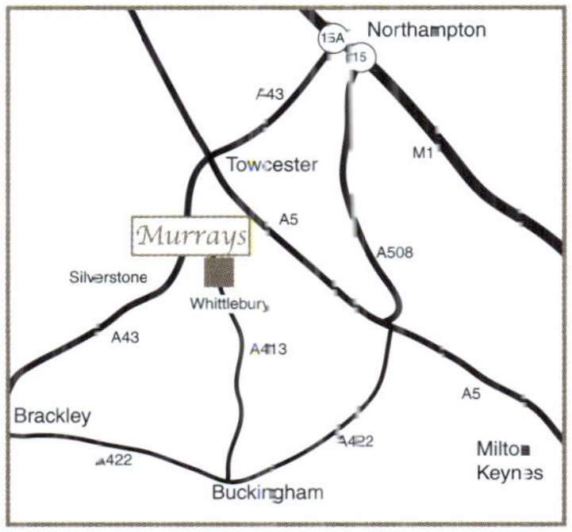

FOODIE Reader Comment

"Wow!!! Amazing food! New and exciting tastes - fabulous service too!"
S. Walker

Food served times
Tue - Sat 7.00 pm - 9.45 pm

£5 10%

The Red Lion

36 Bridle Path, Brafield-on-the-Green, Northants NN7 1BP
Tel: 01604 890707
Email: redlionbrafield@tiscali.co.uk

FOODIE
Reader Comment

"The food and surroundings are second to none - brilliant!"
H. Alders

Tucked away in the beautiful Northamptonshire countryside, "The Red Lion" is very much the heart of Brafield-on-the-Green and only fifteen miles from Milton Keynes.

Manager Laura Croxford has put her stamp on this delightfully located country bistro pub, with the launch of an exciting new food menu, featuring traditional pub classics, tempting chef's specials and a range of mouth watering vegetarian dishes.

The emphasis is on presenting fresh, seasonal, and importantly locally sourced ingredients served in an intimate and informal atmosphere by staff who believe in good old fashioned customer service.

In a recent review in its weekly Dining Out Guide (June 6, 2008), the Northampton Chronicle & Echo awarded "The Red Lion" five stars for both food and service. "Let's not beat about the bush here. This was the best dining experience we've had in Northamptonshire for some considerable time," said the reviewer.

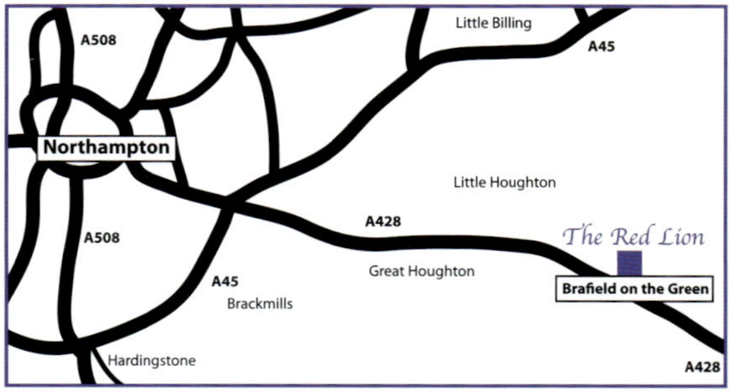

Food served times:
Mon-Thur 12.00 pm - 3.00 pm & 6.00 pm - 9.00 pm
Fri-Sat 12.00 pm - 3.00 pm & 6.00 pm - 9.30 pm
Sun 12.00 pm - 4.00 pm & 6.00 pm - 8.00 pm

£5

The Old Talbot

77 Watling Street
Potterspury
Nr Towcester
Northants
NN12 7QD
Tel: 01908 542124

FOODIE
Reader Comment

"Great menu, wonderful food and family friendly"
S. Johnson

Situated directly alongside the A5 just a couple of miles from Stony Stratford you will find The Old Talbot. This traditional village pub is now in the capable hands of chef/owner Mark and his wife Carol. This enthusiastic couple have big plans and with over twenty years experience in the business you can expect good food together with caring attention.

Mark insists on using good quality produce, which is mostly bought locally to ensure fresh dishes, which are prepared on site daily. From the Inglenook fireplace to the large, beautiful garden complete with a safe childrens corner this is one of those places that you find it hard not to stop at as you drive along the road. This is a family friendly place, so absolutely perfect for Sunday lunch or to celebrate something special with parties of up to 35 people easily catered for.

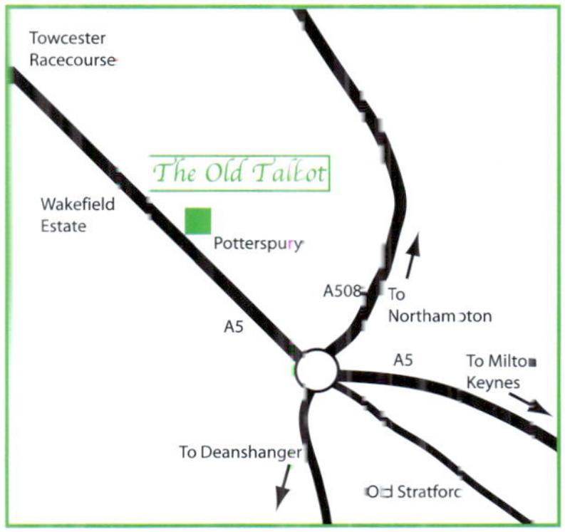

An under-cover smoking area is provided outside. Please note that the 10% discount voucher is accepted between Monday and Thursday only.

Food served times:
Mon - Fri 12 noon - 2.00 pm & 6.00 pm - 9.30 pm
Sat 12 noon - 9.30 pm
Sun 12 noon - 5.00 pm

Vouchers accepted Mon - Thurs only 10%

THE DINING ROOM

82 Derngate
Northampton
NN1 1UH
Tel: 01604 230166
Email: info@thedining-room.co.uk
www.thedining-room.co.uk

The Dining Room is a stunning homage to locally sourced, seasonal free range foods with every dish homemade and lovingly prepared.

A stylish boutique-style restaurant serving breakfast, light meals and hot lunches.

The pièce de résistance – the reinvention of the classic afternoon tea.

Private dining and corporate hospitality.

Decorated in a black and white minimalist style that perfectly complements its surroundings.

An independent business located within The Charles Rennie Mackintosh Galleries.

Opening times:
Tues-Sun 10.00 am - 5.00 pm
plus Bank Holiday Mondays

The Red Lion Hotel

Main Street
East Haddon
Northants
NN6 8BU
Tel: 01604 770223
Fax: 01604 770767

FOODIE
Reader Comment

"Great food in a relaxed country environment"
J. Hills

Now under new ownership The Red Lion Hotel & Restaurant can be found in the very peaceful village of East Haddon, Northamptonshire.

Owners Nick Bonner and Ren Aveiro head up a very competent team of five full time chefs who prepare from scratch all the dishes served from their extensive menu using fresh locally sourced produce whenever possible.

Here you will find mouth-watering traditional dishes on offer such as; Braised Pork Belly with Crispy Crackling; Toffee Apple and Honey Roasted Parsnips; Fillet of Smoked Haddock with Welsh Rarebit and Slow Roasted Thyme Tomatoes; deliciously fresh Chocolate Pavlova with Strawberries and Raspberries and Amaretti Trifle.

The Red Lion has a warm and welcoming feel and its owners are justifiably proud of their efficient but friendly service.

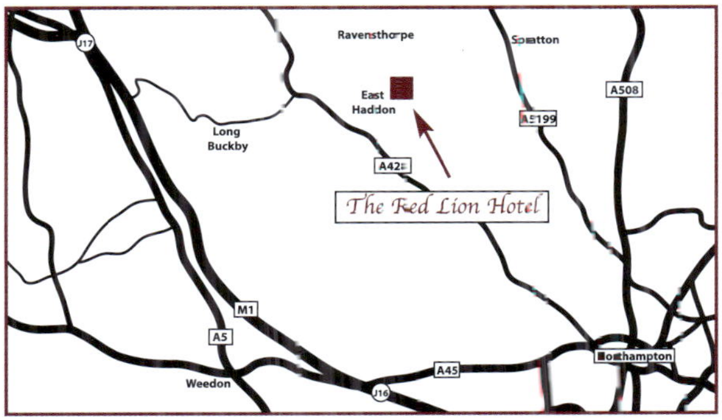

Food served times:
Mon-Sat 12.00 pm - 3.00 pm & 6.00 pm - 10.00 pm
Sun 12.00 pm - 9.00 pm

Congratulations . . .

The winners of THE FOODIE AWARD 2008 are:

St Helena for Bedfordshire

The Plough at Wavendon for Buckinghamshire

Just 32 for Hertfordshire

Murrays at Whittlebury Hall for Northamptonshire

This year you have voted these restaurants your favourites throughout the four counties and Ms L. Godfrey from Northamptonshire has been lucky enough to have her name drawn as the winner of our 2008 prize draw. She will be treated to a meal for two at The Plough at Wavendon.

Well done everyone and thank you to those who have taken the trouble to vote, it really does means a lot!!

The Navigation Inn

Crispy Pork Belly

Chef Profile

Describe your style of cooking

For The Navigation Inn bar menu I go for a simple approach using seasonal ingredients. I source as many things as I can locally. Nearly everything on the menu is made in our kitchens. I try to avoid using ready made items wherever possible.

What dish are you most proud of?

The Butternut Squash and Goats Cheese Lasagne has been a massive success. It's hugely popular and not just with vegetarians. Customers often ask me for the recipe.

No counting the food, what would you say is the most important factor when eating out?

The quality of service can make or break the whole dining experience. As a chef it can be very frustrating when you work hard to produce fantastic food only to be let down by poor service.

What are your thoughts on awards such as Michelin Stars?

Michelin Stars are what I dream about. Having worked in Michelin starred environments I know that is where my true passion lies. With plans for my fine dining restaurant starting to move forward. In the coming years hopefully Michelin stars will be a reality not just a thing of dreams!

How would you like to see the British food industry developing?

It's moving in the right direction - but too slowly. Nationally, Pubs and Restaurants need to raise their standards and get back to making their own food to develop chefs with cooking skills and passion and get away from pre-packed food that just needs heating up.

Dan Cameron

In The Kitchen

Ingredients - Serves 6-8

- ½ Belly of Pork, skin scored, ribs removed, about 2kg *(free-range organic, preferably rare breed)*
- Light Olive Oil
- Sea Salt
- Freshly Ground White Pepper
- 2 tsp Ground Cumin
- 2 tsp Smoked Paprika
- Bunch of Thyme *(leaves stripped)*

Method

1. Rub plenty of salt into the skin side and rest for 1 hour.
2. Pre-heat oven to 220ºc/Gas 7. Wipe salt off and dry well. Rub cumin, paprika and thyme into flesh side.
3. Place pork skin side down on a lightly oiled roasting tray and bake roast for 30 mins. Reduce the temperature to 180ºc and cook for a further 1½ hours.
4. Turn the belly over so it is now skin side up. Be careful not to damage the skin. Return to the oven till the skin is nice and crispy - about 20 mins.
5. Leave to rest for 15 mins before carving.

This dish is great used as a substitute for a joint as a Sunday roast.

Chef Profile

Describe your style of cooking.
Overall, I aim to deliver the quality of Michelin level food, but in a simpler style, as achieved by chefs such as Simon Hopkinson.

What dish are you most proud of?
Dishes that customers consider difficult, but can be made by almost anyone with a little teaching – whether a hot soufflé or a perfectly cooked piece of fish.

Not counting the food, what would you say is the most important factor when eating out?
A great ambience. Service is important, but doesn't need to be formal. Eating out is about bringing people together and having a good time.

What interests do you have outside the kitchen?
Being a father – running our business from home enables me to spend more time with my kids. I also love music and finding bargains at car boot sales.

Who has had the most influence on your career?
Raymond Blanc: His creativity in combining tastes and textures is inspirational, as is his passion for fresh, flavourful produce.

What are your thoughts on awards such as Michelin Stars?
As the 'Oscars' of our industry they stand as a benchmark for quality and help raise awareness of the skill and dedication chefs put into their work.

How would you like to see the British food industry developing?
Small, individual producers getting the opportunity to earn a living growing and producing great food. It's up to us as consumers to seek them out and support them.

Stephen Bulmer

Brook Hall Cookery School

In The Kitchen

Ingredients - Serves 2

For the Cherry Sauce
- 25 ml Red Wine
- 25 ml Ruby Port
- 150g Fresh Cherries *(stoned)*
- ½ pinch of Five-Spice Powder
- 1 pinch of Freshly Ground Cinnamon *(or best quality Ready Ground Cinnamon)*
- Sea Salt & Freshly Ground Black Pepper

For the Duck
- 2 Organic or Free Range Duck Breasts *(Trelough or Barbary)* about 225g each, off the bone
- Sea Salt & Freshly Ground Black Pepper

For the Sweet Potato
- ½ Sweet Potato, about 200g peeled and cut lengthways into slices 10mm thick *(you will need only the 2 largest slices)*
- 1 tsp Groundnut Oil *(or other good unscented oil)*
- 5g Unsalted Butter
- Sea Salt & Freshly Ground Black Pepper

Method

1 *For the Cherry Sauce:* Pre-heat the oven to 180°C/350°F/Gas Mk 4. On a high heat, in a medium saucepan, boil the red wine and port until reduced by half. Add the cherries, five-spice powder, cinnamon, a pinch of black pepper and a pinch of salt. Return to the boil and simmer for 2-3 minutes, then remove 20 cherries and set aside.

2 Pour the remaining cherries and sauce into a blender and blend for 2 minutes. Strain through a fine sieve into a small saucepan, add the reserved cherries to the sauce, then taste and adjust the seasoning if required.

3 *For the Duck and Sweet Potato:* With a very sharp knife, score the skin of each duck breast 6 or 7 times; be careful not to cut the flesh. Season the duck breasts with 2 pinches of salt and 2 pinches of pepper.

4 On a medium low heat, in a large ovenproof frying pan, cook the duck breasts skin-side down to melt the fat away and to crisp the skin for 10 minutes; spoon out excess fat that the duck will produce 2 or 3 times during the process of cooking. Turn the duck on to its flesh side and sear for 1 minute to seal the juices inside. Turn the duck breasts skin-side down again and place in the hot oven for 6 minutes. Remove from the oven and allow to rest for 4 minutes.

5 While the skin of the duck is rendering, on a medium heat, in a large ovenproof frying pan, fry the sweet potato slices in the groundnut oil and butter. Colour them for 4-5 minutes on each side, seasoning with 2 pinches of salt and 2 pinches of pepper, then transfer the pan to the oven for 5 minutes to finish the cooking. Serve each duck breast on a slice of roasted sweet potato, with the hot cherries and cherry sauce spooned around.

Brook Hall Duck with Cherries

Crooked Billet

Easy Cheesecake

Chef Profile

Describe your style of cooking

Regional, fresh, in season and something you would not necessarily get at home.

What is the most unusual request you have had from a diner?

A mother brought in Turkey Twizzlers and asked if we could cook them as her child would eat nothing else. We refused and gave the child pan-fried strips of guinea fowl. The child said it was the best chicken they had ever eaten.

Not counting the food, what would you say is the most important factor when eating out?

The company - and looking at the positives; I want to enjoy the food not criticise it.

If you weren't a chef what occupation would you like to have?

Comedian.

Who has had the most influence on your career?

Sally Clarke; she taught me seasonal food and the positives of British cuisine.

What are your thoughts on awards such as Michelin Stars?

If you could ask any of the guides, especially Michelin, what you have to do to win accolades: they all say the same thing. "Cook for your customers and the rewards will come".

How would you like to see the British food industry developing?

I would like to see supermarkets and other chefs refrain from selling foreign produce. Support your local farmer and British food.

Emma Gilchrist

In The Kitchen

Ingredients

- 8 Digestive Biscuits
- 35g Melted Butter
- 250g White Chocolate
- 125g Double Cream
- 2 Punnets fresh Raspberries, English please!!!

Optional Easy Raspberry Sauce

- 1 Punnet of Raspberries
- 2 tbsp Caster Sugar
- Juice of One Lemon

Method

1. Crush the digestives and combine with the melted butter.
2. Divide the mix into 4 and press into 4 metal rings. If you do not have rings a cake tin or pie dish is great.
3. Place the white chocolate in a glass bowl and melt over a pan of hot water, stirring occasionally.
4. When the chocolate has melted add the cream and stir.
5. Gently fold in most of the raspberries, retaining some for a garnish.
6. Pour the mixture into the rings or cake tin. Allow to cool and refrigerate.
7. When needed remove from the ring or tin, place a few fresh raspberries on top and serve.

Optional Easy Raspberry Sauce

1. In a food processor blitz all the ingredients together.
2. Strain through a sieve and serve.

Chef Profile

Describe your style of cooking

An eclectic style of European cuisine with the cooking being clean and honest with the emphasis on fresh produce.

What dish are you most proud of?

Baked Peppered Halibut in Greek Yoghurt (this keeps the fish lovely and moist).

What is the most unusual request you have had from a diner?

Mmm...strange requests; we once had a lady complain that the crust on our white chocolate bread & butter pudding was a bit hard!! - as she was drumming her spoon on the terracotta pot it's cooked in. We are regularly handed unwrapped babies nappies - for our pleasure maybe!!

What is your favourite local restaurant? (other than your own)

Our daughter is a nightmare eater, so Wagamamas is hers, so now our family favourite. We do love a good curry, The Jaipur in Milton Keynes is our favourite.

Not counting the food, what would you say is the most important factor when eating out?

It's a subtle blend of relaxed atmosphere with quiet efficiency; the ability to make customers feel at home.

If you weren't a chef what occupation would you like to have?

Years ago when your occupation was on your passport I always wanted something that sounded romantic; Tree Surgeon, Stunt Man. Four generations of my family are in the art world, so maybe something in that field.

Who has had the most influence on your career?

Rick Stein is one of my favourites, his simplicity of ingredients and the feeling he really enjoys life.

Mark Hickman

Moreteyne Manor

In The Kitchen

Ingredients - Serves 4

- 4 x 150g Cod Fillets
- 50g Butter
- 50g Olive Oil
- 50g Paprika
- 4 Medium Courgettes
- Baby Vine Tomatoes
- Capers
- Chopped Chives
- Seasoning
- Herb Vinaigrette

Method

1. Roll the cod fillets in the paprika until covered then lightly season.
2. Heat half the oil and butter in a large flat pan, place the cod fillets top side down in the hot fat.
3. Allow the cod fillets to cook for 1 minute then gently turn the cod once, then cook for a further 1 minute.
4. Place under a medium heat grill to finish cooking for 3 to 4 minutes.
5. Using a peeler, peel thin slices from the courgettes.
6. Heat the remaining oil and butter in a large flat pan or wok, quickly stir-fry the ribbons of courgette noodles for 1 - 2 minutes.
7. Halve the baby vine tomatoes, season and warm under grill for 1 - 2 minutes.
8. Divide the noodles on to four warm plates then place the cod fillets on top of the courgettes.
9. Serve the warm baby tomatoes and capers around the cod. Finish with a herb vinaigrette and chopped chives.

Paprika Cod on Courgette Noodles

Horse & Jockey

Crispy Pork Belly with Roasted Root Vegetables

Chef Profile

Describe your style of cooking.
Rather than adhere to one style I believe a Chef should continually evolve. My aim is not to be stuck in one place and to seek to give the customer the best experience every time.

What dish are you most proud of?
Our own Smoked Pigeon Breast with Beetroot and Horseradish Relish.

What is the most unusual request you have had from a diner?
Once asked if I could buy the local pub of a customer so they did not have to travel so far.

What is your favourite local restaurant (other than your own)?
The Black Horse at Ireland, Nr. Shefford.

Not counting the food, what would you say is the most important factor when eating out?
Style, ambience and good friendly service and of course, beautiful toilets!

What interests do you have outside of the kitchen?
Rough shooting, working and training my two gun dogs and deep sea fishing.

If you weren't a chef what occupation would you like to have?
Fruit and Hop Grower or Gamekeeper.

Who has had the most influence on your career?
My Mother. She could burn peas and turn tenderloin into leather, so it was self-preservation that I learnt to cook. Sorry Mum!

How would you like to see the British food industry developing?
I hope that we will see more high quality, original and unique outlets.

Darron Smith

In The Kitchen

Ingredients - Serves 4

- 2 kg Pork Belly - Bone In
  (The better the breed of pig the more crispy the skin)
- 2 pinch Maldon Salt
- 2 pinch Cracked Black Pepper
- Olive Oil
- 4 large Carrots cut into 4
- 2 large Parsnips cut into 4
- 1 Swede *(roughly cut)*
- 8 Baby Beetroot *(leave whole)*

Method

1 Score the skin of the pork.
2 Rub with olive oil and sprinkle with the salt and pepper.
3 Place in roasting tray in middle of oven for 1¾ hours at 180ºc.
4 Whilst pork is cooking blanch vegetables (beetroot separately) and drain when soft.
5 Place in roasting tray and coat with olive oil and sprinkle a pinch of salt and pepper over vegetables.
6 Cook for 1 hour at 180ºc.
7 After 1¾ hours raise oven to maximum and cook pork for further 15 mins.
8 Leave to rest for 5 mins out of oven.
9 Cut into 4 and serve surrounded with vegetables and sauce of your choice.

Chef Profile

Describe your style of cooking.
Modern English

What dish are you most proud of?
All of them!

What is your favourite local restaurant?
(other than your own)
The Angel Inn, Long Crendon.

Not counting the food, what would you say is the most important factor when eating out?
Service and environment.

What interests do you have outside the kitchen?
Hunter gatherer and martial arts.

If you weren't a chef what occupation would you like to have?
Gamekeeper or farmer.

What are your thoughts on awards such as Michelin Stars?
They are not my thing, I just want to produce well cooked fresh local produce and be consistent with it.

How would you like to see the British food industry developing?
I would like to see more fresh local producers used and to be rid of microwave kitchens doing boil-in-the-bag food.

The Carriage House Restaurant

Jason Caple

In The Kitchen

Ingredients - Serves 4

- 175g Butter
- 240g Plain Flour
- Pinch of Salt
- 2 Egg Yolks

- 250g Rowan Goats Cheese
- ½ bunch of Chives
- Zest of 1 Lemon
- Pinch of Salt
- Freshly Ground Pepper
- 7 Sunblush Tomatoes

- 100g Black Olives
- Shallots
- Zest & Juice of 1 Lemon
- 50ml Olive Oil
- 2 sprigs of Thyme
- ½ bunch of Chives
- 1 Garlic Clove

Pre-heat oven to 180°c/Gas 4-5

Method

1 Chop butter and place in a mixer with flour and salt then mix. 2 When mixture resembles crumble add the egg yolks and mix till it forms a dough. Mould into a flat piece then wrap and chill for 20 mins.
3 When chilled roll out to about 3mm thick and cut into four 4" circles. Place into buttered tart cases, line with cling film and put rice on top, fold in cling film and blind bake for 15-18 minutes. When cooked leave to cool.
4 Place goats cheese in mixer with roughly chopped chives and grated lemon zest. Blend until all ingredients are mixed. The cheese should look slightly green. 5 Remove from mixer and chill until needed.
6 Place olives, shallots, garlic, lemon zest, juice and herbs in a food processor until roughly chopped, add olive oil, seasoning and mix until combined.
7 Take cheese mixture from fridge, level fill pastry case, place spoonful of olive mixture over the top so cheese is fully covered. Fan the sunblush tomatoes on top and place on baking tray on greaseproof paper and bake for 3-4 minutes at 180°c/Gas 5 until slightly warm. 8 Serve with dressed wild rocket.

Goats Cheese Tart

The Carrington Arms

Lemon Crusted Scallops with Black Pudding, Pea Purée & Beetroot Compote

Chef Profile

Describe your style of cooking.
Modern British - classic dishes with a twist!

What dish are you most proud of?
Our twist on Coronation Chicken as a main course with a salad of raisins, pancetta and pine nuts. A modern twist on a classic.

What is the most unusual request you have had from a diner?
"I'm Lactose intolerent....I'll take the ice cream please!!"

What is your favourite local restaurant? (other than your own)?
The Crooked Billet.

Not counting the food, what would you say is the most important factor when eating out?
The wine list.

What interests do you have outside of the kitchen?
Watching and playing sport of any kind and eating out (I like to have others cook for me!).

Who has had the most influence on your career?
My chef lecturer, Richard Ferrier from Birmingham School of Food... preached classical French cuisine but a true culinary genius.

What are your thoughts on awards such as Michelin Stars?
Over-priced and over-complicated food. You can get just as well cooked dishes for a third of the price in a good modern bistro pub.

How would you like to see the British food industry developing?
Self-sustainable restaurants that grow their own organic produce for better quality and flavour.

Jamie Norman

In The Kitchen

Ingredients - Serves 1

- 100g Scallops *(or 3 in number)*
- 50g Black Pudding *(cut into rings)*

For the Pea Purèe

- 50g Frozen Peas
- 25g Diced Potato
- Sprig of Mint
- 1tsp White Wine Vinegar
- 200ml Vegetable Stock
- 1 tsp Icing Sugar

For the Beetroot Compote

- 1 Beetroot Bulb
- 15g Diced Potato
- 50ml Red Wine
- 50ml Red Wine Vinegar
- 50ml Water

For the Crust

- ¼ Lemon Zest
- Sprig of Lemon Thyme

Method

1. ***For the Pea Purée:*** Boil peas and potato with sprig of mint until peas are aldente.
2. Remove mint leaves, strain peas and blitz in a blender, adding pea stock slowly. Finish with white wine vinegar and icing sugar.
3. ***For the Beetroot Compote:*** Peel and dice beetroot, bring to boil in red wine, red wine vinegar and water.
4. Strain, blend beetroot, adding beetroot stock slowly. Pass through a sieve.
5. ***For the Scallops:*** Chop lemon thyme through lemon zest, add salt and pepper and crust one side of each scallop.
6. ***To serve:*** Pan fry black pudding until slightly crisp.
7. Crisp crust side of scallops in pan, then sauté in butter.
8. Place pea pureé at three points, topped with black pudding and scallops, then dress with beetroot compote and endive leaves.

Chef Profile

Describe your style of cooking.
Our menus deliver exciting English food with Italian and French influence using the best ingredients from Europe. There is something for everyone.

Not counting the food, what would you say is the most important factor when eating out?
Warm hospitality and atmosphere it is the whole experience that counts. You can have a good eating experience in the simplest of cafes or delis to the finest multi starred restaurants it is the attitude and care of the whole team that makes the difference.

What interests do you have outside the kitchen?
I love motor sports and am very interested in cars. I often cook Sunday lunch with the sound of Formula 1 in the background.

Who has had the most influence on your career?
I have been lucky enough to spend my career working in quality establishments with some of our industries most interesting and most influential people. There are so many people have helped to shape my career; Raymond Blanc, Paul Heathcote, John Hoskins, Paul Caddy, Marc Veyrat, Peter Allen, my wife ...... I meet interesting people all the time they may not be famous but they all have something to offer and you never stop learning.

What are your thoughts on awards such as Michelin Stars?
We have been fortunate enough to be written up by some of the many guides and were pleased to recently be recognised by the Which? Good Food Guide as the Restaurant of the Year for 2008. What is most important to us is that the guides recognise us as a restaurant that is looking after its customers consistently well. Hungry travellers consult guides to choose a good place to eat and the guides rely on those places to be as good as the last meal they had. We genuinely cook for our customers and we try never to let them down.

Martin Lee

The Plough Restaurant at Bolnhurst

In The Kitchen

Ingredients

- 6 Single Muscle Haunch Venison Steaks (We use Fallow deer from Denham Estate in Suffolk)
- 500 ml Roasted Chicken Stock
- 500 ml Veal or Demi Glaze

For the Venison Sauce
- 6 Shallots
- 2 Cloves of Garlic
- Sprig of Thyme
- 50ml Good Quality Red Wine Vinegar
- 6 Peppercorns
- 1 Bay Leaf
- 300ml Red Wine
- 500ml Roasted Chicken Stock
- 500ml Veal Stock or Demi Glaze

Method

1 *For Venison Sauce*: Slice shallots and garlic and sauté until shallots are soft and caramelised, allow 10 minutes slow frying. 2 Deglaze the pan with red wine vinegar and continue cooking until the liquor has evaporated. 3 Add peppercorns, bay leaves and red wine, bring back to the boil and reduce liquid by two thirds. 4 Add brown chicken and veal stock and reduce until sauce consistency. 5 Strain through a chinoise or fine sieve.

1 *For Venison Steaks*: Heat char grill/pan until hot. 2 Lightly season & brush with olive oil. 3 Cook on hot char grill turning regularly to char all the sides. Cook to preference 4-8 minutes from rare to medium. 4 Carve the steak against the grain.

Venison is available all year round. Cook broad beans and young beetroot and light crème fraîche potato in the spring/summer. In the winter it is great with slow braised red cabbage and rich fondant potato.

Denham Estate Venison Steak and Red Wine Sauce

Jusr 32 Restaurant

Chicken Mousse Wrapped in Parma Ham served with a Truffle & White Wine Sauce

Chef Profile

Describe your style of cooking
Modern British with a serious hint of French and influences from the East.

What dish are you most proud of?
Duo of Wild Salmon and Dover Sole layered with Duxelles Mushrooms, Tomato Fondue and a Pernod scented cream sauce.

What is your favourite local restaurant (other than your own)?
I like to visit London restaurants, my most recent being 'Morgan M' and the experience was fantastic.

Not counting the food, what would you say is the most important factor when eating out?
Friendly staff and relaxing atmosphere.

What interests do you have outside of the kitchen?
Cooking with friends at home. I also play a lot of sports and enjoy running. I ran in the 2005 London Marathon and was proud to finish in 4hrs 18 mins.

If you weren't a chef what occupation would you like to have?
I would like to be a tour guide and travel the World.

Who has had the most influence on your career?
My cookery teacher in St Nazaire, France.

How would you like to see the British food industry developing?
To use more local and original produce and to promote the regions where you work and live.

Eric Huvelin

In The Kitchen

Ingredients - Serves 4

- 600g Pork Fillet
- 8 Slices Parma Ham
- 100ml Chicken Stock

For the Stuffing

- 100g Chicken Breast *(roughly chopped)*
- ½ Egg White
- 100ml Double Cream
- 10 Fresh Sage Leaves
- Salt & Pepper

For the Sauce

- 2 Small Shallots *(finely chopped)*
- 150ml White Wine
- ½ Litre Reduced Chicken Stock
- ½ tsp Truffle Paste

Method

1. Place chicken breast with sage, salt and pepper into food processor and mix, add egg white and double cream and mix quickly for no more than 20 seconds.
2. Open up pork fillet to form rectangle.
3. Spread mousse mixture onto pork fillet then roll lengthwise, cover the outside with Parma ham. Wrap tightly with cling film and leave to chill in fridge for 2-3 hours.
4. To make sauce, place shallots and wine in saucepan and reduce liquid by ⅔rds. Add chicken stock and simmer for 4-5 minutes. Press sauce through fine sieve then add truffle paste and salt and pepper to taste.
5. Remove cling film from pork and cut into 8 portions. Seal in a hot pan with oil then add 100ml of chicken stock, place into oven (electric 230° or gas mark 8) and cook for a further 10 minutes and check that it is cooked through.

We served this with a fondant potato, braised celeriac, baby carrots, French beans and decorated with a sprig of deep fried sage (as photograph). Enjoy and bon appetit!

Chef Profile

Describe your style of cooking
Simple British.

What dish are you most proud of?
Our pies. We don't do crock-pots so all our pies are made in large dishes and served straight on to the plate.

What is the most unusual request you have had from a diner?
A raw fillet steak served with a raw egg and tabasco sauce.

Not counting the food, what would you say is the most important factor when eating out?
The staff.

What interests do you have outside of the kitchen?
Golf and skiing whenever possible.

If you weren't a chef what occupation would you like to have?
Captain of a cruise ship has always appealed to me.

What are your thoughts on awards such as Michelin Stars?
I think they reward a great deal of effort but ignore the fact that the majority of people can't afford to eat out at the prices Michelin Star restaurants have to charge.

How would you like to see the British food industry developing?
I would like to see people turn away from large chain brewery pubs and restaurants and the pre-portioned boil-in-the-bag food they serve.

The Old Talbot

Mark Jones

In The Kitchen

Ingredients - Serves 8

- 8 Egg Whites
- 14oz Caster Sugar
- Strawberries
- ½ tsp Baking Powder
- Fresh Cream

Method

1. Whisk 8 egg whites until they peak.
2. Add half the sugar and whisk thoroughly.
3. Add remaining sugar and baking powder and whisk until you could turn the bowl upside down without the mixture falling out.
4. Shape using two spoons onto a metal tray covered with greaseproof paper.
5. Bake in the oven for 1 hr 20 mins at 110°c.
6. Turn oven down to 100°c for a further 20 mins.
7. Turn off the oven and leave the meringues inside for approx 1 hr.
8. Serve with fresh strawberries and double cream.

Meringue with English Strawberries

The Tewin Bury Restaurant

Red Berry Panacotta and Brittany Farm Shortbread

Chef Profile

Describe your style of cooking
Classical French with a Mediterranean influence and a British twist.

What is the most unusual request you have had from a diner?
To cook a 2 course meal for a man's pet dog!

What is your favourite local restaurant? (other than your own)
Auberge du Lac.

Not counting the food, what would you say is the most important factor when eating out?
Ambience, quality of service and attention to detail.

What interests do you have outside of the kitchen?
Scubadiving, photography and jogging.

If you weren't a chef what occupation would you like to have?
A professional scubadiver.

Who has had the most influence on your career?
Michael Trama, Patron chef at L'Aubergade in Agen, France (currently has 3 Michelin Stars).

What are your thoughts on awards such as Michelin Stars?
Great to have, stressful to keep. Too many restraints.

How would you like to see the British food industry developing?
At the moment there is too much from around the world to promote "British food" in a healthy manner and keep to it.

Benoit Jarvery

In The Kitchen

Ingredients - Serves 4

For the Biscuit:
- 300g Flour
- 200g Brown Sugar
- 90g Egg Yolk
- 3g Salt
- 220g Butter

For the Panacotta:
- 150g Sugar
- 960ml Double Cream
- 200ml Full Fat Milk
- 10-12 Gelatine Leaves
- 1 Punnet of Berries
- A dash of Rum
- Sugar to taste

Method

1. ***For the Biscuit:*** Mix butter and flour until crumb-like.
2. Mix egg yolk and sugar together, add the salt.
3. Mix no.1 and no. 2 together and leave to set in the fridge. When cool roll and cut into a round shape. Cook at 180ºc for 10 minutes.
4. ***For the Panacotta:*** Bring cream, milk and sugar to the boil, add gelatine leaves. Put in a mould and leave in a fridge to set for 24 hours.
5. ***For the Red Berry Compote:*** Mix red berries with a dash of rum and add icing sugar to taste.
6. When panacotta has set for 24 hours, mould it and set it on top of a biscuit. Decorate it with mint and red berry compote....Enjoy!

Chef Profile

Describe your style of cooking.
Modern and classical British with international influences.

What dish are you most proud of?
I would not say one single dish but the separate daily seafood menu has been a unique point for us and enables me to focus on my passion for fish and seafood.

Waht is the most unusual request you have had from a diner?
Asked to boil a fillet steak in water to medium - never really found out why!

Not counting the food, what would you say is the most important factor when eating out?
Without a doubt, service - like food it can make or break your night out.

If you weren't a chef what occupation would you like to have?
I worked in the live music industry for a while and would have loved to have managed a place like The Astoria in London.

Who has had the most influence on your career?
I had a manager called Richard Evans who was hugely influential - other than that - my mum and especially my dad.

What are your thoughts on awards such as Michelin Stars?
They are suitable for certain types of restaurants but it is often about creating a perception and playing the game - not always about just good food.

How would you like to see the British food industry developing?
More accessible sources and fewer hypocrites in the industry as a whole. Good food must be available at prices people can afford.

Chris Spencer

The Wollaston Inn

In The Kitchen

Ingredients - Serves 4

- 1-2 kg Wild Sea Bass
- 24 Green Olives
- 24 Crayfish Tails (cooked)
- 8 Chestnut Mushrooms
- 200g Pancetta (diced)
- 20 New Potatoes
- 200g Spinach
- 80g Butter
- 1 Fennel
- 60ml Olive Oil
- Juice of one Lemon

Method

1. Fillet the Sea Bass and cut fillets in half for four portions.
2. Cook new potatoes for 10-12 minutes in boiling water then slice and leave to dry.
3. Heat 2 non stick frying pans.
4. Slice fennel and mushrooms.
5. Add olive oil to both pans, season flesh of fish with salt and pepper then place in pan flesh side down. Cook on medium heat for 5 minutes, add butter to pan then turn fish over, add lemon juice then set to one side.
6. Add mushrooms and pancetta to other pan, cook for 30 seconds then add sliced potatoes and fennel. Cook for one minute, turn potatoes then add butter, olives, crayfish tails and spinach. Add butter, season mix then turn out onto plates. Place Sea Bass onto mix and garnish with fresh dill.

Sea Bass with Sautéed Mix

Verney Arms

Chocolate Fondant

Chef Profile

What is your style of cooking.

Modern British food with European influences.

What dish are you most proud of?

I would have to say I am most proud of the freshly baked bread. It is a simple but effective way to convey what's to come.

What is your favourite local restaurant? (other than your own)

We do not tend to eat out that much other than take-away, but the local curry house in Winslow is a favourite.

What interests do you have outside of the kitchen?

I love to play golf when I have the time, as well as having a go on my drums.

Who has had the most influence on your career?

Without question, my Dad. He gave me the desire to succeed, along with the right work ethics.

If you weren't a chef what occupation would you like to have?

Probably something to do with music.

What are your thoughts on awards such as Michelin Stars?

I have always said Michelin Stars are great if you can get them, but sometimes it's who you know instead of what you know.

Lee Anstee

In The Kitchen

Ingredients - Serves 6

- 185g Dark Chocolate
- 185g Butter
- 3 Eggs
- 3 Egg Yolks
- 90g Sugar
- 20g Flour

Heat oven to 200°C / Gas Mark 6

Method

1. Melt the butter and chocolate in a bowl over a pan of simmering water until well combined. Take care not to burn the chocolate.
2. Whisk together the eggs, yolks and sugar.
3. Gradually add the chocolate mixture to the eggs and sugar until well combined.
4. Sieve the flour into the chocolate mixture and gently fold in.
5. Pour into 6 well buttered ramekins and bake in a pre-heated oven for 7-8 minutes.
6. The fondants can be turned out onto a plate or served in the ramekins with crème fraîche.

Note: The fondants should be cooked on the outside with a soft centre.

Chef Profile

Describe your style of cooking
Modern European food.

What dish are you most proud of?
At the moment, Aylesbury Duck and Foie Gras Terrine; Rhubarb, Pistachio and Watercress Salad.

What is the most unusual request you have had from a diner?
"Can I have a quiet table on a Saturday night?"

Not counting the food, what would you say is the most important factor when eating out?
Good company, good surroundings, professional service and good wine.

What interests do you have outside the kitchen?
I have a young family so spending as much time as I can with them. The children have a lot of interests and that keeps us busy.

If you weren't a chef what occupation would you like to have?
It would have been great to get paid for racing motorbikes. Failing that, something to do with construction.

Who has had the most influence on your career?
My father, Patrick O'Keeffe was a great chef. I spent many years under his guidance. He gave me a great foundation to build on. We still use a lot of Patrick's recipes today.

How would you like to see the British food industry developing?
It would be nice to walk into any restaurant in the country and know that you are going to get a decent meal.

Jonathan O'Keeffe

In The Kitchen

Ingredients - Serves 4

- 4 Slices Smoked Salmon
- 4 Slices Brioche
- 6 Eggs Whisked & Seasoned
- 300ml Double Cream
- 50g Butter
- 100g Crème Fraîche
- Black Pepper
- 1 Lemon

Method

1. Boil the cream and butter in a non-stick frying pan and reduce by half.
2. Toast the Brioche.
3. Meanwhile, stir in eggs to cream and butter using a spatula. Keep moving the egg mix till nearly cooked.
4. Place toasted Brioche slices on plates, put scrambled eggs on top, cover with smoked salmon then top with crème fraîche.
5. Serve with ground black pepper and a squeeze of lemon - don't forget the glass of champagne!

The Kings Head, Ivinghoe

Smoked Salmon and Scrambled Eggs

Murrays, Whittlebury Hall

Crab Cocktail with Crab Toasties and Avocado Ice Cream

Chef Profile

Describe your style of cooking.
I always find that a hard question to answer but I would have to say modern British with classical and international influences.

What dish are you most proud of?
Currently the Crab Cocktail is the one I am most happy with.

What is the most unusual request you have had from a diner?
Sometimes we receive requests for very strange combinations of food but these remain secret.

Not counting the food, what would you say is the most important factor when eating out?
To feel relaxed and to be able to just sit back and enjoy the experience.

What interests do you have outside of the kitchen?
I enjoy football, although there is not a lot of time for much else.

If you weren't a chef what occupation would you like to have?
A creative occupation; perhaps a DJ.

What are your thoughts on awards such as Michelin Stars?
I think they are good for benchmarking but you can sometimes lose focus chasing accolades. I believe a good business with happy returning customers is the best reward and recognition you can get.

How would you like to see the British food industry developing?
I would like to see more local produce being used and for Britain to become more of a self-sufficient seasonal country.

Kevin Barron

In The Kitchen

Ingredients

For Crab Jelly
- 1 pint Crab Stock
- 7 leaves Gelatine

For Crème Fraîche Crab
- 200g Freshly Cooked White Crab Meat
- 4 spoonfuls Crème Fraîche
- Salt & Pepper
- Juice of 1 lemon
- Half bunch Chives (finely chopped)

For The Toasties
- 8 Slices Ciabatta Bread Toasted
- 150g Freshly Cooked White Crab Meat
- 1 tbls Crème Fraîche
- Half bunch Spring Onions
- Salt & Pepper
- 2 Egg Yolks

For Avocado Ice Cream
- 565ml Milk
- 200ml Whipping Cream
- 3g Salt
- 5g Silk Gel
- 3 Avocados

Method

1. Soak the gelatine in water until soft. Warm the crab stock then mix in the gelatine until dissolved, pour through a fine sieve and pour into martini glasses leaving enough room at the top of the glass for the crab mix. Chill until set.
2. Mix the 200g of crab with the juice, crème fraîche and chives, season to taste. Once the jelly is set, carefully spread a layer of crab across the jelly and leave to chill.
3. For the toasties, mix the 150g of crab with the egg yolks, spring onions and crème fraîche. Spoon equally onto the bread and grill until golden brown.
4. Place all the ingredients for the ice cream in a blender and blitz and churn until set (add 50g of sugar if it sets too hard).
5. Scoop or quenelle the ice cream, place on top of the cocktail. Garnish with watercress and serve with the toasties on the side.

Chef Profile

Describe your style of cooking

Good honest food - what you see is what you get. One of my customers once described it as "old school - but new". I think they were trying to say traditional with a modern take.

What dish are you most proud of?

This spring we served double roasted shoulder of lamb. It was just fantastic; simple but packed full of flavour and one of those dishes which people seem not to cook at home anymore. I'm big on using the less fashionable cuts and making something worthwhile out of them. I had lots of positive comments back from the restaurant.

What is the most unusual request you have had from a diner?

To entertain a group of girls on a hen party. I declined, my chef whites were staying firmly on my person.

What is your favourite local restaurant? (other than your own)

Moore Place Hotel. There always seems to be something a bit different and 'quirky' on the menu, be it a new combination of flavours or a completely new ingredient.

Not counting the food, what would you say is the most important factor when eating out?

The welcome and service you receive. Doesn't matter what's on the menu, if you don't feel comfortable you could be eating the best food ever but not enjoy the experience.

What are your thoughts on awards such as Michelin Stars?

I think recognition for what you do is important and something you can aspire to in any career. I like the type of awards that recognise the informal but excellent establishments which are accessible to the average diner.

Mark Wood

The Plough at Simpson

In The Kitchen

Ingredients

For the Pork
- 450g Pork Tenderloin
- 1 Eating Apple
- 3 Large Potatoes
- 1 Bulb of Garlic
- 2 Savoy Cabbage Leaves
- 1 Leek *(cut lengthways to make 'sheets')*

For the Sauce
- 1 Cooking Apple
- 1 Clove of Garlic
- 1 Medium Onion
- 300ml Vegetable Stock
- Salt & Pepper to season
- 25g Unsalted Butter

Method

Pre-heat oven to 220°c/Gas 7

For the Stuffed Pork
1. Blanch cabbage leaves and 'sheets' of leek.
2. Butterfly pork and stuff with sliced apple and wrap blanched leek sheets around pork, then the cabbage leaf and finally bacon. Tie with string to keep secure. Cool in fridge for 30 minutes.
3. Place pork in top of oven for 20 minutes, when cooked allow to rest before serving.

For Roasted Garlic Mash
1. Cut garlic bulb in half, drizzle with olive oil and roast for 20 minutes until soft.
2. Prepare and boil potatoes until soft.
3. Remove cooked garlic cloves from skin, add to potatoes and mash, adding seasoning and butter to taste.

For the Sauce
1. Peel and chop apples, garlic and onion. Fry in a little butter until soft.
2. Add water and reduce by half, add a final knob of butter to thicken sauce, remove from heat.

Stuffed Pork Tenderloin on Garlic Mash with Apple Sauce

The Bricklayers Arms

Grappes Bread & Butter Pudding

Chef Profile

Describe your style of cooking.
Modern French/British food with Latin twist.

What dish are you most proud of?
I am very proud of my home smoked fish.

What is the most unusual request you have had from a diner?
A full Scottish meal with recipes from the 19th Century.

Not counting the food, what would you say is the most important factor when eating out?
Service!!! Not as a spotless or faultless service but just nice and friendly with a smile.

What interests do you have outside of the kitchen?
Gardening, Kayaking and spending as much time as possible with my family.

If you weren't a chef what occupation would you like to have?
I love nature so I think I could have done anything to do with wildlife and outdoor activities.

Who has had the most influence on your career?
Being born into a family mad about food for generations and having the chance to learn the basics from pastry to butchering since I was very young, I would say everything came naturally.

How would you like to see the British food industry developing?
I really would like to see apprenticeships coming back or really good catering schools to encourage young chefs to be passionate about food and teach them the basic knowledge of food.

Claude Paillet

In The Kitchen

Ingredients - Serves 8

- 1 kg Mixed Grapes
- 1 Vanilla Stick
- ½ litre Milk
- ½ litre Cream
- 200g Sugar
- 8 Whole Eggs
- ½ Loaf of White Bread *(crust removed)*

Method

1. Boil the milk and add the bread in pieces with one vanilla stick cut through the middle.
2. Add the cream and simmer for an extra 5 minutes.
3. Whisk the eggs and sugar together then add to the bread and milk.
4. Remove the vanilla stick and add the washed grapes.
5. Pour the mixture into a tray and bake for 1 hour at 140°c.
6. Let it cool down slightly and serve warm with cream coulis, custard or ice cream....enjoy!

Chef Profile

Describe your style of cooking
Modern British with French influence.

What dish are you most proud of?
Duck Breast Medium Rare with a Pumpkin Gratin.

What is the most unusual request you have had from a diner?
I don't have anything very excentric yet but seen some very strange allergies.

Not counting the food, what would you say is the most important factor when eating out?
Service with a smile.

What interests do you have outside of the kitchen?
Water Polo and Horse Riding in Summer and Frisbee Player.

If you weren't a chef what occupation would you like to have?
Maybe a fashion designer.

Who has had the most influence on your career?
My friend and chef Claude Paillet.

What are your thoughts on awards such as Michelin Stars?
It helps chefs aim to make their cooking standards one step higher.

How would you like to see the British food industry developing?
Developing more of our old favourite dishes.

Alan Bell

The Nags Head

In The Kitchen

Ingredients - Serves 8
- 75g Butter
- 75g Flour
- ½ Litre Milk
- 4 Egg Yolks
- 10 Egg Whites
- 2 Whole Eggs
- 150g Cheese
- 10g Butter for dish
- 10g Salt & Pepper
- Nutmeg

Pre-heat oven to 220°c/Gas 7

Method
1. Take a souffle dish or 8 individual ramekins and brush with 10g butter and flour.
2. Melt the 75g butter in a small pan and add the flour, cook for 2 minutes stirring continuously. Add the milk, salt, pepper and nutmeg and then whisk until it boils. Add 4 yolks, 2 whole eggs and cheese.
3. In a bowl whisk the egg whites with a pinch of salt until very firm. Add half to the first mixture and then the other half very carefully.
4. Pour the mixture into the ramekins and cook for 10 minutes at 220°c and then turn the oven down to 180°c and cook for a further half an hour. If using a large dish add on 5 minutes to the first setting and then 15 minutes to the second. Serve straightaway. As an alternative; add some ham or cooked mushrooms. Enjoy!

Cheese Souffle

The Plough, Wavendon

Chocolate Studded Cape Malva Pudding

Chef Profile

Describe your style of cooking

Classical French, combining the best of the New World with the attention to detail of the Old.

What dish are you most proud of?

My marinated tuna with samphire. The Japanese call it Umame and they're absolutely right!

What is the most unusual request you have had from a diner?

(Whilst in Cape Town) To serve the lobster, still alive, on a board with a knife. Apparently he wanted fresh sashimi of lobster tail.

What is your favourite local restaurant? (other than your own)

The Waterside Inn, Bray. Elegance in food, service and ambience.

Not counting the food, what would you say is the most important factor when eating out?

Service. The levels of service and attention to detail will determine whether you return as a diner or not. Price becomes irrelevant.

Who has had the most influence on your career?

Master Chef Bill Stafford M.O.G.E. An amazing chef, under whom I was privileged to train and work for when I lived in Cape Town.

How would you like to see the British food industry developing?

Expensive prices for food are here to stay. Less influence from the supermarkets and their diktats; more influence from Slow Food and local producers; more experimentation from the average consumer of food - getting to understand food and how wonderful it is to be surrounded by quality produce and then being able to cook it simply. The back to basics approach.

Grant Hawthorne

In The Kitchen

Ingredients - Serves 4

For the Sponge

- 80ml Whole Milk
- 100g Double Zero Flour
- 160g Granulated White Sugar
- 1 Pinch of Salt
- 8g Bicarbonate of Soda
- 2 Whole Eggs
- 30g Smooth Apricot Jam
- 15g Melted Butter
- 15ml Red Wine Vinegar
- 120g 70% Chocolate *(for studding)*

For the Syrup

- 200g Granulated White Sugar
- 140g Butter
- 80ml Water
- 80ml Milk
- 320ml Double Cream

For the Coffee Custard

- 2 Egg Yolks
- 25g Caster Sugar
- 125ml Double Cream
- 125ml Whole Milk
- 50ml Espresso

Assembly

- Fresh Blackberries
- Picked Mint Sprigs
- 4 x Caramel Baskets

"This dessert is a lighter version of the local Sticky Toffee pudding and is a speciality from Cape Town. The sublime sweeter tastes of the sponge are offset by the addition of the imported bitter chocolate and marry well with the coffee custard or Vanilla pod ice cream."

Method

1 *For the Sponge:* Sieve all dry ingredients. Make a well and add the eggs. Add the melted butter, jam and vinegar. Add the milk. Reserve to one side. Line a greased and floured baking dish (deep). Bake at 200°c for 30 minutes. Remove briefly from the oven and stud the sponge with the chocolate pieces. Return to the oven for a further 10 minutes.

2 *For the Syrup:* Bring to the boil in a separate pot. Reserve to one side. Pour gently over the hot sponge and leave to soak for approx. 20 minutes. Chill until set. Divide into four portions.

3 *For the Coffee Custard:* Whisk the egg yolks and sugar over Bain Marie. Heat the milk and incorporate into the egg. Return the mixture to a saucepan and cook over a low heat until thick. Allow cooling, reserve to one side.

4 *Assembly:* When reheating, caramelise the Malva in oven (220°c) for 6-8 minutes. Serve warm with a small pool of coffee custard or rich vanilla ice cream (pictured). Garnish with fresh berries, mint and sugar basket (optional).

Chef Profile

Describe your style of cooking

Fresh / Plentiful / Traditional.

What dish are you most proud of?

Simple fresh battered fish and chips or a real Sunday lunch.

What is the most unusual request you have had from a diner?

"Could I have the cream of tomato soup with an infusion of rosemary, without the rosemary please?!"

Not counting the food, what would you say is the most important factor when eating out?

Service, without a doubt, guests must be greeted and treated in a happy, polite manner.

If you weren't a chef what occupation would you like to have?

Anything that involves making people smile. I've been told with my quick wit I should be on the stage.

Who has had the most influence on your career?

Gordon Ramsay - I like his style, he keeps it fresh and simple and if he thinks someone is a prat he tells them.

What are your thoughts on awards such as Michelin Stars?

I won't pay to achieve an award! Food that is exceptional should sell itself.

How would you like to see the British food industry developing?

It's gone full circle over the past 20 years. I never thought I would see a prawn cocktail again, but it's still popular. You just need to serve home cooked fresh produce. Traditional, well cooked food will always be popular.

Alan Drake M.B.I.I.

The White Hart, Grafton Regis

In The Kitchen

Ingredients

- 2 Eggs
- 2 tsp English Mustard
- 1 pint Vegetable or Olive Oil
- 2 tbsp Vinegar (approx)
- Pinch Salt & Pepper

With the so called "Credit Crunch" I have decided this time to do a money saving recipe. It frustrates me so much when I see people buying Mayonnaise and dips etc. It's so easy to do, the only thing you need is a food processor. Remember that thing you have stuffed away at the back of the cupboard you never use?!

Method

1. Set up the food processor with the bowl and blade for mixing/chopping.
2. Crack the 2 eggs into it, add the mustard, salt and pepper. Replace the lid on machine.
3. Turn on the food processor and using a measuring jug, pour in approximately half the oil, you must pour as slowly as you possibly can, adding a drop at a time, add the vinegar and continue to add the rest of the oil, again as slowly as you can (if you add the oil too quickly the mayonnaise will split and curdle). You should now have basic mayonnaise.

Try these other options by adding a few more ingredients to the mayonnaise. ***Salad Cream***: just add a little more mustard and a drop more vinegar for a delicious salad cream. ***Garlic Dip***: just add a few cloves of garlic and a few herbs (either: parsley/oregano/basil/rosemary). ***Prawn Cocktail Sauce (Marie Rose)***: add a drop of ketchup, a pinch of paprika and a very little pinch of chilli powder. ***Tartare Sauce***: add a large gherkin, a few capers and some parsley for a great accompaniment to fish (remember the water/vinegar content in this and add less vinegar to the original mayonnaise). Remember, this is made with fresh eggs and needs to be kept in a refrigerator and will keep for 4-5 days.
Good luck and happy dipping!

Simple Mayonnaise and Dips

fine foods and wines

15 Cornwall Place
High Street
Buckingham
Buckinghamshire
MK18 1SB
t: 01280 817 141
e: info@thehalibut.co.uk
www.thehalibut.co.uk

halibut

FISHMONGER TRAITEUR RESTAURANT

2 Course Set Lunch £12.00 3 Course Set Lunch £15.00 2 Course Set Dinner £21.00 3 Course Set Dinner £26.00

Opening times:

Fishmonger	Tues to Sat	9am - 5pm
Traiteur	Tues to Sat	11am - 5pm
Restaurant	Tues to Sat	
	Lunch.	Noon - 3pm
	Dinner.	6pm - 10pm

Located in a smart paved precinct in the heart of historic Buckingham, Halibut delivers the ultimate seafood experience by way of a Fishmonger, Traiteur and Seafood Restaurant

The Fishmonger

A cornucopia of high quality fresh fish and crustacea prepared to order by friendly specialists happy to offer advice and suggestions.

The Traiteur

Everything is hand-made by us on the premises using fresh, carefully sourced ingredients. From exotic salads inspired by the foods of the mediterranean to our renowned luxury jumbo fishcakes, all dishes are available to take away, making us the ideal choice for dinner parties, catered events, picnics and BBQ's .

The Restaurant

The first floor at Halibut is home to a chic and intimate eatery where the freshest seafood and simple, skilful preparation let the flavours of the fish shine through. From traditional staples such as fish & chips to lesser known exotics such as Tilapia and Barramundi, Halibut is the perfect choice for corporate entertaining and special occassions as well as an everyday neighbourhood eatery

For larger dinners and intimate events to be remembered, the fully licensed restaurant at Halibut is also available for exclusive hire for groups of up to 30 people **We also host special events and tasting days. Please see the website for details.**

Everyone in Milton Keynes deserves Waitrose

Manor Road
Brackley
Northants NN13 6BE

Meadow Walk
High Street
Buckingham
Bucks MK18 1RS

13 Bowen Square
Daventry
Northants NN11 4DR

3 Leyton Road
Harpenden
Herts AL5 2TJ

The Lairage
Bedford Road
Hitchin
Herts SG5 2UG

9 Waterborne Walk
Leighton Buzzard
Beds LU7 1DH

728 Midsummer Boulevard
Central Milton Keynes
Bucks MK9 3NJ

1 Ermine Close
Mayne Avenue
St Albans
Herts AL3 4JZ

Richmond Road
Towcester
Northants NN12 6HZ

Come to Waitrose on Midsummer Boulevard and share in its passion for food and reputation for excellent customer service. Its offer of quality products, honestly priced within a spacious environment makes food shopping a pleasure.

No matter what your taste, cooking talents or time constraints, there's something for everyone. With dedicated food counters - delicatessen, salad, patisseries, cheese, fish and meat - boasting only the highest quality foods, there's a huge choice to be had.

With Cheese, Fish and Meat Specialists at the counters, you can ensure you'll get not only the best selection of produce to choose from, but also the finest advice - whether that be for everyday eating or party planning.

Waitrose

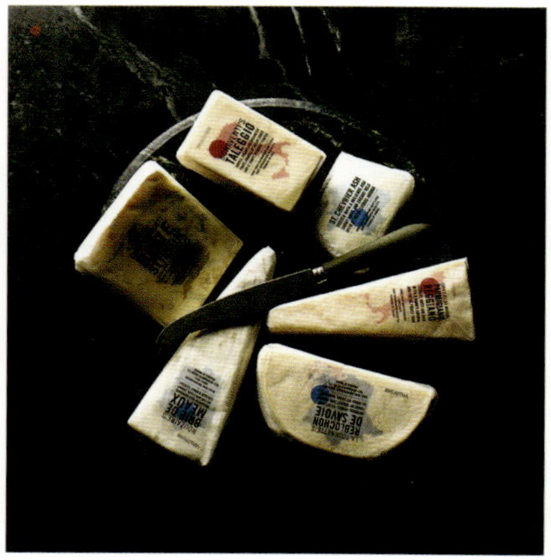

For the perfect wine, take a trip to Milton Keynes and make the most of its fine wine selection. Having won a whole host of medals and trophies for their wines, there's something for every taste, every meal and all occasions at Waitrose.

As healthy eating is such a hot topic at the moment, it's great to have a range of foods, such as Waitrose Wholesome, that are both easy to choose - and use - on a daily basis. Containing 140 simple, inherently nutritious foods including nuts, seeds, cereals, grains, dried fruits, beans and pulses, the range is ideal for both food lovers and the health conscious alike.

And with a range of excellent services available such as Waitrose Entertaining, Waitrose Deliver and Quick Check, there's more to Waitrose Milton Keynes than meets the eye. For more information on these services, visit www.waitrose.com

Best Butchers Ltd

Unit 5
Lower Rectory Farm
Great Brickhill
Milton Keynes
MK17 9AF
Tel: 01908 375275
Email: bestbutchers@btconnect.com
www.thebestbutchers.co.uk

Quality, variety and a commitment to personal service sum up Simon Boddy's "Best Butchers Ltd".

This absolutely spotless shop was opened in 1994 on a working organic farm and specialises in supplying locally sourced meat. Besides joints and cuts of beef, lamb, pork and poultry the shop is renowned for its fine pork, beef and lamb sausages all prepared on the premises along with bacon, dry-cured and slowly smoked over beech. Air-dried then smoked, Brickhill ham is Simon's own adaption of Parma ham and to complement this, a fine selection of English and Continental cheeses. Fish lovers will be pleased to learn that on Fridays and Saturdays, Simon along with Liz Fryer, source direct from Billingsgate market all the fresh fish and then expertly prepare it for you to enjoy.

Acclaimed by Rose Prince of the Daily Telegraph that the air-dried coppa was the best air-dried meat she had tasted in Britain and also rated in the Sunday Observer as "Best Deli".

Opening times:
Mon-Fri 8.00 am - 5.00 pm **Sat** 8.00 am - 2.00 pm

THE GATEWAY TO REAL VILLAGE SHOPPING

BATTLERS GREEN FARM

RURAL SHOPPING VILLAGE & TEAROOMS

TAKE A BREAK & PAY A LEISURELY VISIT TO HERTFORDSHIRE'S UNIQUE BATTLERS GREEN FARM

In this lovely farmyard setting you'll find over a dozen traditional stores including the long-established **Battlers Green Farm Shop** with its superb range of high quality food and wines, as well as other prestigious retailers including **Aga** and **Fired Earth** showrooms, a fishmongers, a butchers, a pet shop, a gift shop and a holistic shop to name but a few. While you're here be sure to take a relaxing break in our spacious and distinctive tearooms, **The Bull Pen**. There's ample free parking so why not make a day of it?

BATTLERS GREEN FARM • COMMON LANE • RADLETT • HERTFORDSHIRE • WD7 8PH
TELEPHONE: 01923 856551 • WWW.BATTLERSGREENFARM.CO.UK

Just half a mile off the B462 (Radlett/Watford Road) take the New Road turning at the mini roundabout and we are half a mile on the right hand side.

BATTLERS GREEN FARM SHOP THE LOOSE BOX DYNATIQUE THE FLOWER GROVE DESTINY MAINE SAIL LALINE ANDREW BROWN HOME BRIMARK BUTCHERS CLASSIC FRAMING THE AGA SHOP FIRED EARTH THE BULL PEN TEA ROOMS REALLI-SKI SIMULATOR

River Nene

www.rivernene.co.uk

our farm organic vegetables on your table

We all like to impress in the kitchen. There's nothing better than the greedy scramble across the table for seconds (and sometimes thirds!) when you've cooked a great meal. But to create food that warrants extra helpings, you need the best ingredients. You can't always get the crispest salad leaves, the juiciest tomato or the crunchiest apple from the supermarket. Often it has been flown around the world to get there, losing its flavour along the way.

River Nene grows more than 100 varieties of organic fruit and vegetables on its farms, all carefully chosen for their flavour. River Nene's organic fruit and veg is freshly picked on the farm and delivered free to customers' doors by the shortest possible route. With not a limp lettuce in sight. From the simplest salad to a fragrant curry, with an organic veg box you'll create meals that outshine the ordinary. And River Nene's website is bursting with recipe ideas for days when you need inspiration.

The organic box scheme is easy and flexible, with a choice of different sizes and contents to suit you and the things you like to cook. Order weekly, fortnightly or as a one off, and switch between boxes and extras whenever you want. You can top up your order with organic milk, cream, eggs, chocolate, wine and more. Just make enough for seconds.

Organic veg boxes start from just £8.35

For more information see **www.rivernene.co.uk** or call **0845 078 6868.**

DELICATESSEN ESTRELLA

2A High Street
Winslow
Buckinghamshire
MK18 3HF
Tel: 01296 712466
www.delicatessenestrella.co.uk

Located in the heart of the pretty market town of Winslow, right opposite the Market Square, Delicatessen Estrella specialises in providing the highest quality foods and ingredients to bring you the flavours of the Mediterranean. Helen and John Knight have a passion for all food but especially that of Spain and North Africa and always stock an excellent range of unusual Spanish products, including charcuterie and cheeses.

Throughout the shop the emphasis is always on food of the highest quality, which they source from the best suppliers in their fields, including cheeses from Neals Yard Dairy and Spanish meats from Brindisa. Delicious home cooking is always on offer, a range of coffees are ground to order and fresh artisan bread is available several days a week.

Estrella opens every Friday night until 7pm to make it easy for busy workers to pick up a one stop meal. This might range from a tapas selection or an antipasto plate to a cheese board, cake or pudding. Complement your food with their selection of wines and sherries, or try a few bottles from their popular range of locally brewed real ales.

So if you are a lover of good food looking for the best products and ingredients for yourself, or you're looking for a food or drink related gift such as a basket or hamper made to order, make sure you visit Delicatessen Estrella.

Opening times:

Mon-Thur 10:00 – 17:30
Fri 10:00 – 19:00
Sat 09:30 – 17:00
Sun (Jun, Jul, Aug and Dec) 10:00 – 13:00

Country House Fine Foods & Catering

Unit 1
The Old Farmyard
Castle Ashby
Northamptonshire
NN7 1LF
Tel/Fax: 01604 696742
Email: traceymurray67@hotmail.com
www.countryhousefinefoods.co.uk

Tracey Murray and Clive Jackson took over the ownership of Country House Fine Foods in March 2008. The small independent delicatessen is unique in its setting and atmosphere.

The shop enjoys an idyllic setting situated in the rural shopping yard in the picturesque village of Castle Ashby the ancestral home of the 7th Marquis of Northampton and is less than 30 minutes drive from Milton Keynes.

Selling quality specialist foods from around the world and United Kingdom the new owners are keen to support local and small rural businesses. The range of food on offer is chosen for its quality and originality, Artisan cheeses, fine delicatessen counter, the shelves groan under the weight of the fine chutney's and preserves. Fine wines including a selection of fair trade, and small local brewery beers are all available. Having an enviable reputation for homemade dinner party foods, picnic and BBQ accompaniments specialising in succulent dressed Salmon, and divinely decadent desserts and celebration cakes, which few can resist. These can be ordered through the shop allowing you to enjoy your entertaining.

Country House Picnics
A Country House recyclable picnic box with table cloth will make your visit to Castle Ashby hassle free, available in three sizes for 1 to 4 people these can be pre-ordered or prepared for you on the day by their own staff.

Country House Catering
They offer stylish and flexible catering to ensure a day to remember. Food is freshly prepared from the finest ingredients in their own kitchens. Traditional wedding cakes or cheese stacks designed to suit your requirements. Business lunches, corporate functions, hand made canapes, dinner parties and family celebrations are a speciality.

Country House Hampers
A Country House Hamper makes the perfect gift for every occasion offering a sublime treat for food lovers everywhere. Bespoke hampers and good food gifts, designed with careful attention to detail. Both local and national delivery service available.

Opening times:
Tue-Sat 10.00 am - 5.00 pm
Sundays and Bank Holidays 11.00 am - 5.00 pm

Situated off the A428 Bedford to Northampton road near Yardley Hastings.

FT **O**

Padbury Meats

Main Street
Padbury
Buckingham
MK18 2AY
Tel: 01280 823366
Email: thompson433@hotmail.co.uk
www.padburymeats.co.uk

A traditional butcher and family business established over 25 years ago, we are proud of the exceptional service and quality we offer to our customers.

Located in the heart of the village of Padbury, close to the market town of Buckingham, our reputation for providing the very finest farm-reared meat, poultry and local produce has made us the butcher of choice for numerous businesses, pubs, restaurants and schools in Buckingham and the surrounding area.

We are always happy to offer advice and guidance on the best cuts of meat for particular dishes, to prepare joints on or off the bone, or to select prime game or poultry for special orders, we cater for every requirement from Sunday roast for the family to a celebratory occasion.

By scouring the local area, we are able to give our customers much greater choice, as well as offering the traditional favourites. For the more adventurous, and those who enjoy experimenting in the kitchen, you'll find an impressive stock of herbs, spices and condiments, and we are constantly discovering new delicacies and ranges to tempt and satisfy the most discerning of tastes.

Very much a family oriented business, we strongly believe in convenience and value, although we adopt a rather different approach to the big supermarkets. Rather than being pre-packed and difficult to inspect, our meat is well-displayed giving you free range to browse and make your choice. Being locally produced, it has not been transported a great distance which means it's exceptionally fresh and tender when it reaches your table.

For busy mums with young children there is ample parking directly outside our door making it quick and easy to pop in to do your shopping. And if you're too short of time to bake your own, simply pick up one of our delicious freshly made cakes for afternoon tea.

Opening times:
Mon-Fri 7.00 am - 5.00 pm **Sat** 7.00 am - 1.45 pm

Browns of Stagsden FARM SHOP

Manor Farm
High Street
Stagsden
Bedford
MK43 8SQ
Tel: 01234 822330
Email: jpeterbrown@btinternet.com
www.brownsofstagsden.co.uk

The Brown family has farmed in and around Bedfordshire for many years, and three generations are now involved in the business. The family has always taken great pride in growing crops and rearing cattle, pigs and turkeys, so they decided to open a shop at Manor Farm, in the beautiful village of Stagsden.

The shop has now been trading for three years and is enjoying an ever increasing customer base, proving it to be a much appreciated source of home and locally grown produce.

Traditional breeds of cattle, pigs and turkeys are reared for the shop using home-grown grain where possible, whilst lambs and free range chickens are reared locally. Game is also available when in season. All sausages, burgers and ready meals are prepared on site and you will also be able to buy local vegetables, cheeses, hams, organic flour, fresh bread, gluten-free cakes, free range eggs, local milk, ice-creams and tempting accompaniments.

In the run up to Christmas - a very busy time of the year for Browns - you will be able to pre-order your home-reared turkey and any other meats, or choose from our wide range of hampers which make for excellent presents.

So if you are looking for something different and enjoy good quality produce, please pay the shop a visit, where our helpful staff will offer you a warm welcome.

Opening times:
Tue-Thur 9.00 am - 5.00 pm
Fri 9.00 am - 6.00 pm
Sat 9.00 am - 4.00 pm
Fresh fish every Saturday 9.00am - 1.00 pm

Aubergine Fine Foods

73 High Street
Woburn Sands
Bucks
MK17 8QY
Tel: 01908 582020
Email: auberginedeli@btconnect.com

Aubergine Fine Foods is an independent, family-owned delicatessen in Woburn Sands, established by local residents Jill and John Goulding. Run by food lovers for food lovers, Aubergine strives to offer international speciality foods alongside the finest locally-sourced produce.

The ever expanding range includes British and continental cheeses, salamis and chorizos, pastas, cooking sauces, preserves, chocolates, breads and biscuits, plus all the kitchen cupboard essentials. Fresh fish is available to order direct from Billingsgate Market three times a week.

Wherever possible Aubergine sources foods from local, small-scale producers, including free-range eggs from Cranfield; bacon, sausages and hams from their butcher's own farm in Bedfordshire; bread from Ampthill; organic milk from Flitwick; plus honey, vegetables and delicious home-made cakes from Woburn Sands itself.

In addition, there is an increasing range of 'free from' foods for people with special dietary requirements, including gluten-free pastas, cereals and biscuits. Aubergine is also an ethical and environmentally responsible business. Many products are fairly traded, offering producers in the developing world a better deal, and all the shop's own packaging is bio-degradable, recyclable, or from a sustainable source.

Latest developments include a new lunch menu offering pasta dishes, filled ciabatta rolls and gourmet salads, plus great coffee and fresh fruit smoothies. A business and event menu is also available with free local delivery. And for those of you looking for something a bit different for your wedding or special event, a cheese 'wedding cake' or tower of cheese makes a spectacular and original centrepiece.

Whatever your culinary tastes, if you're passionate about food and looking for an alternative to the supermarket experience, pay a visit to Aubergine - your local, independent fine food store.

Opening times:
Mon-Fri 8.00 am - 6.00 pm
Sat 9.00 am - 5.00 pm

A Fresh Approach To Food

Frosts Garden Centre Woburn Sands has been judged a 'Garden Centre of Excellence' by the Garden Centre Association in 2008, and is one of the top 15 Garden centres in the UK. We are developing our award winning centre to offer customers even more reasons to enjoy shopping with us.

The latest phase of our development is the 'Food at Frosts' food hall. We are taking a fresh approach to our offer to bring you the highest quality food, sourced from the best local suppliers.

Designed to meet all of your culinary requirements our range provides a wide variety of exciting and inspirational ingredients and fresh produce, all of which are hand selected to compliment seasonal changes.

The food hall includes fresh fruit and vegetables, a butchers' counter, a wide selection of fresh fish, and a delicatessen with over 50 cheeses. Freshly baked bread, pies and cakes are available every day along with a range of ready meals, dairy products, Jams, preserves and condiments. We also offer a delightful range of confectionery and chocolate to tempt you!

Our food is not the only range selected for taste – we also offer a hand picked selection of wines, ciders and local beers for your enjoyment too!

Frosts Garden Centre Ltd, Newport Road, Woburn Sands, Milton Keynes, MK17 8UE
01908 583511
www.frostsgroups.com

The Shires Spit Roast Catering Company

Specialist Outdoor Caterer

Bairstows Lodge, Watling Street,
Towcester, Northants NN12 8ET
Telephone: 01327 352962
Mobile: 077734 22074
Email: mail@spitroastcompany.co.uk
www.spitroastcompany.co.uk

Corporate events
Weddings
Private parties
Team building
Product launches
Christmas celebrations
Fund raising
Charity Function
Christenings
from 50 - 2000 guests catered for

Equipment hire and sales

BYRMAN
of Roade

1 The Ridings, Roade, Northamptonshire NN7 2NH
Tel 01604 862702 Email byrmans@tiscali.co.uk

Made in our Kitchen by Byrman ...

- Silverside of Beef
- Boneless Leg of Pork
- Turkey Breast
- Honey Roast Ham
- Ham in Golden Breadcrumbs
- Smoked Gammon in Cider
- Byrmans Famous Pate
- Speciality Sausages
- Assorted Steak Pies
- Pasties, Sausage Rolls
- Veggie Pastries
- Coleslaw, Potato Salad
- Filled Rolls ... Made to order

RETAIL
Traditional village shopping for that unbeatable home-cooked taste.

Cooked Meats, Pies and Pastries freshly cooked and baked on the premises along with fresh meat, vegetables and locally baked bread. Fine wines, ciders and ales complement tasty cheeses from our delicatessen.

CATERING
Whilst visiting, discuss with us or email your catering requirements for your party, wedding or business function.
With over 22 years of catering experience, we offer a Complete Catering Service to fit most budgets and we are confident we will be able to help.

Opening times:
Mon-Sat 9.00 am - 6.00 pm

Re-awaken your senses

Rediscover the Joys of eating

Be a part of changing the future for the next generation

A Slow Food dinner can last for hours. Mouth-watering seasonal menus often containing seven delicious courses highlighting local produce and not forgetting the fine wine or cask ales. We view them as a chance to relax, meet new friends and share in a love of food, safe in the knowledge that all profits is helping to…

- Catalogue marginalised foods in danger of disappearing
- Promote local and worldwide artisan producers
- Support Slow Food's University of Gastronomic Sciences

On a local level your money goes towards educating the next generation in the real taste of food. We hold fun educational events for local school children. At these events they learn about seasonal produce, our local food heritage and why they should be proud to eat and understand the journey of our food from the planet to the plate.

Slow Food® Bedford

To find out more and join our community e-mail slowfoodbdford@ntlworld.com, visit our web site www.slowfoodbedford.co.uk or call 07753 780607

COMING SOON TO A DELI NEAR YOU

Local chef prepared dishes brought to you by THE FOODIE Square Guide. . .

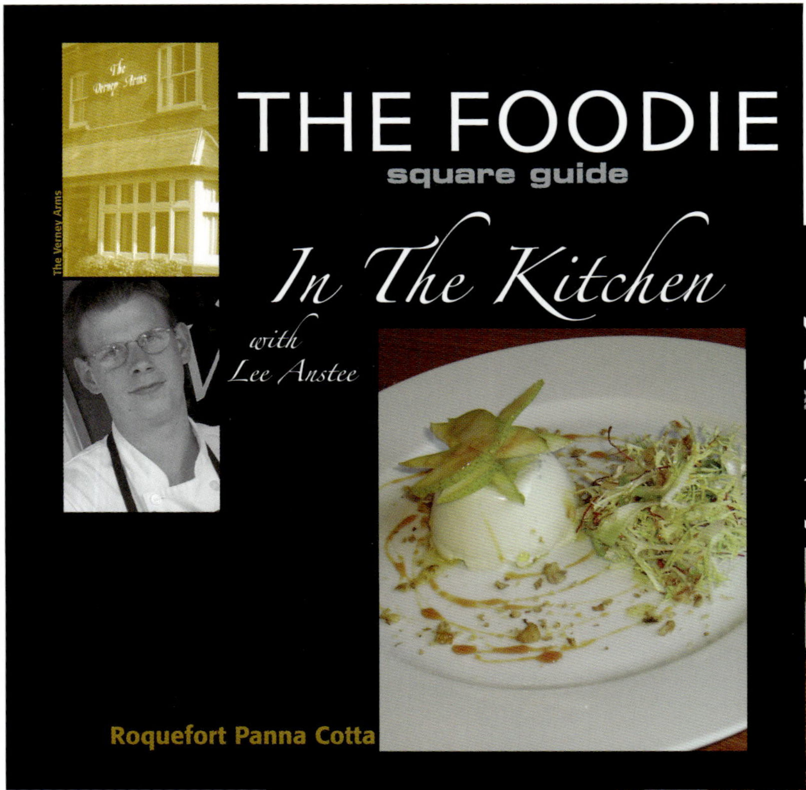

. . . for you to enjoy at home

The dishes shown are for the purposes of this advert only and may not be avaiable within the "In The Kitchen" range.

fine foods and wines

lifestyle

lifestyle

Welcome to CLAYDON

Claydon House was built by the second Earl Verney between 1757 and 1771 and was bequeathed to the National Trust in 1957. Claydon contains some of the most important Rococo interiors in the country and the Chinese Room, the Grand Stairs and the Gothic Room are among the most flamboyant interiors of their era. During the 19th century Florence Nightingale, sister in law to Sir Harry Verney, was a regular visitor.

Telephone number for National Trust House is 01296 730349.

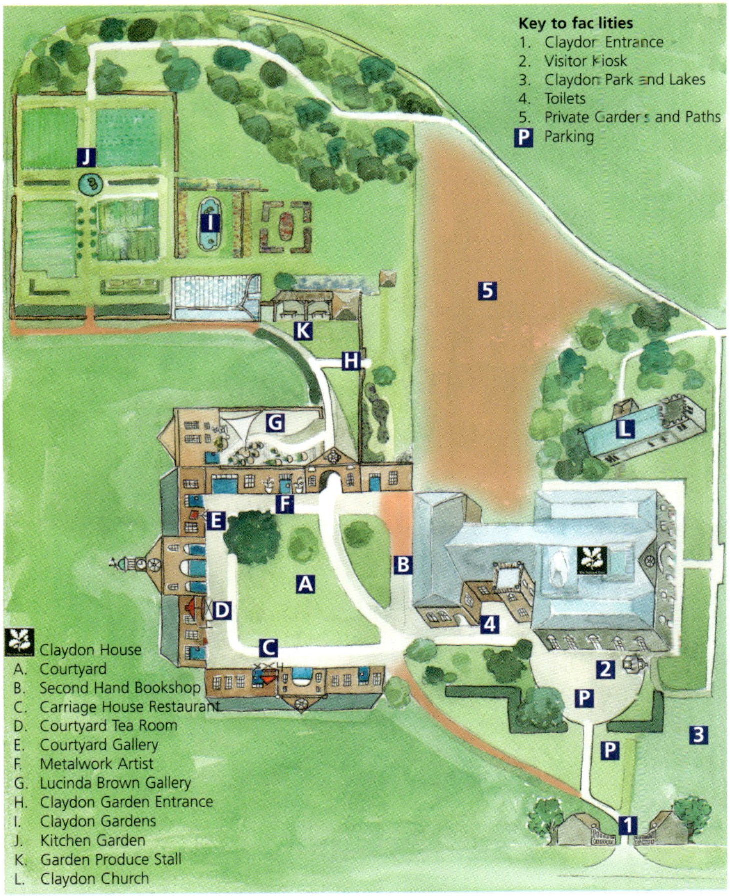

The Carriage House Restaurant/Tea Room C D

At the restaurant relax in beautiful surroundings and enjoy delicious and imaginative dishes created by the Head chef Jason Caple, who prides himself on using local and estate produce.

For details please call 01296 730004
More information at www.thecarriagehouserestaurant.co.uk

The tea room offers light refreshments and a comfortable chair in the Courtyard to relax after visiting the house and other attractions.

The Courtyard Gallery E

The Gallery includes a range of pictures created using different media and ranging from very contemporary to classical in style.

For more information contact Susan Lefebvre on 01296 738090 or 01296 712082

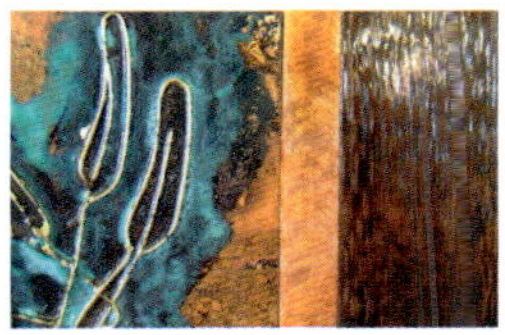

Metalwork Artist F

Kate Edwards trained as a Silversmith and now creates contemporary metal artwork for interior spaces.
Commissions for corporate and private buyers welcome.

Contact details 07879 653855 or www.k8art.co.uk

Lucinda Brown Gallery G

A warm welcome awaits visitors to this wonderful courtyard studio/galllery. Come and see a stunning selection of unique high quality gifts including ceramics, glass, textiles, metal art and jewellery.

For further information visit www.lucindabrowngallery.co.uk or telephone 01296 733984 or mobile 07873 234527

Claydon Gardens H I J K

The Gardens are open from April to the end of October, 12 noon to 5pm, Saturday to Wednesday. A classic example of a Country House walled garden including a productive kitchen garden, selling produce in season.

For further information Tel: 01296 730252, Email: info@claydonestate.co.uk, Web: www.claydonestate.co.uk

For opening dates, times and admission prices, please contact individual attractions.

BEAUTIFULLY

A winning combination...

Oliver James Garden Rooms take the need for extra space and create a beautiful and practical place to spend time all year round. Whether you want a place to play, a place to relax, a place to entertain or a place to eat, you can do it all surrounded by the harmony of your garden.

Why a Garden Room?

You may have decided it would be nice to integrate your house and garden with a Garden Room. You may need to create extra space by adding on to the back of your family house. You may live in a townhouse where extending the property with an ingeniously designed Garden Room is the most practical way of achieving valuable additional space. A Garden Room can be a beautiful and practical way of creating an extra room, a place where you can relax and enjoy the outdoors all year round, but if it is to be a permanent and comfortable part of your home it will need to be carefully designed and constructed.

Oliver James Garden Rooms can provide a variety of solutions to the requirement for extra space. Never too hot or too cold, a Garden Room can be used all year round. The unique design means that you can combine rooms seamlessly or have entire glazed walls to make the most of your space.

Which design is for you?

- Do you need extra space for the children to play?
- Would you like to have a stunning room in which to dine or entertain?
- Would you like to bring your sitting room into your garden?
- Would you like to extend your kitchen and feel like you're cooking outdoors?

Whatever your requirement Oliver James understand how to take your ideas and turn them into a beautiful and practical reality.

What do I get?

Regardless of why you choose an Oliver James Garden Room you can be assured of the following:-

- State of the art folding, sliding doors, which open up to give you an uninterrupted view of your garden, bringing the outside in.
- Hardwood and/or Aluminium frame construction with warm, insulated, and tiled roofs.
- Under floor heating as standard.
- Six years aftercare and guarantee.
- A quote you can rely on with no hidden costs to surprise you later on.
- Trained experienced installers.
- Dedicated project management and support to keep you informed throughout the build, including expertise in obtaining planning permission.
- Full documentation of the works carried out to current building regulations with all the necessary paperwork for your Home Improvement Packs.

What next?

Oliver James will visit you in your home to discuss your requirements. If you have your own ideas they can be used to create a completely individual space. If you want Oliver James to come up with the ideas for you they'll ask you questions about your home and lifestyle to create a solution that's perfect for you. They will also consider the location of your Garden Room and tailor make a solution that lets the most light into the space available. Some solutions have been indulgently high ceilings and stunning lighting combined with top of the range electronic Velux windows that even close themselves if it starts to rain!

TRUST MARK

01908 367177
Visit us at: www.wecreatespace.com

MORGAN GILDER

FINE FURNITURE
INSPIRING INTERIORS

Pay a visit to our showroom to see the latest in design-led upholstered furniture, fabrics and wallpapers.

A wealth of product and advice available to help create your perfect home interior, and all without the hassle of city shopping.

From classic to contemporary, we offer high quality products for the discerning client.

Our upholstery suppliers include Duresta, John Sankey & Henderson Russell and for those looking for cutting edge style and design we offer the full range from Ligne Roset.

Beautiful hand finished window dressings of all styles from swags & tails to roman blinds are created from fabrics by all the leading design houses.

MORGAN GILDER ~ **COME AND BE INSPIRED**

VISIT US AT: 14 HIGH STREET, STONY STRATFORD, MILTON KEYNES, MK11 1AF
OR CALL US ON: 01908 568674

We are an independent co-educational day school with 250 children between the ages of 3-13

The school prides itself on a family atmosphere with a maximum class size of 16 pupils

THE GROVE INDEPENDENT SCHOOL & DAY NURSERY

'To inspire, develop and achieve'

Loughton
Redland Drive
Milton Keynes MK5 8HD
Tel: 01908 690590

www.groveschool.co.uk

Enquiries@groveschool.co.uk

The Grove Nursery provides part and full time day care and education from birth to three

Within a friendly structured environment Monday to Friday 8am - 6pm

VITA

"Vita" offers a range of Italian and Mediterranean inspired dishes and is the hidden gem for dining within G Casino Luton. Our varied menu offers a range of freshly cooked dishes prepared with high quality ingredients.

We cater for groups for all occasions from birthdays to anniversaries so why not enjoy a night to remember in our fabulous restaurant. After you've sampled the delights of Vita, you can give an added twist to your night in this unique environment offering great gaming for everyone from the beginner to the professional! Or why not kick back and relax in our contemporary late night bar and enjoy live music every Friday or Saturday night.

Bookings are recommended to avoid disappointment.

G Casino Luton, 35 Park Street West, Luton LU1 3BE
Telephone: 01582 813780
Guests will be required to register and will need to provide a valid ID - driving licence or passport.

HELPING YOU · STAY IN CONTROL ·
www.gambleaware.co.uk

G CASINO

THE DAY SPA
WHITTLEBURY HALL
A new way to Day Spa
For information on our latest spa offers
call us on 0845 400 0002
(Quote Foodie)
or visit www.thedayspa.co.uk

73

The £10 gallon is imminent

£2.25 per litre

Be ahead of the rest and prepare yourself and your business before it happens!

With careful analysis of your requirements a bespoke plan will reduce the impact of this inevitable occurrence.

(Oh - and don't worry . . . we'll not be trying to sell you a Toyota Prius!)

Central Leasing

Central Leasing Ltd • Duck Lane • Woburn • Milton Keynes MK17 9PT
t: 0870 4100004 • f: 0870 4100005

FSB network a LeasePlan Brand

74

Paula Stevens

ghd

REDKEN 5TH AVENUE NYC

At Paula Steven's Hair Studio we have created an atmosphere of friendly professionalism. A place where you can come in and relax, knowing that you are in good hands.

BICESTER
5 Nightingale Place
Langford Village
01869 247261

BUCKINGHAM
3A Meadow Row
Buckingham
01280 817701

ZSL
WHIPSNADE ZOO
CHEETAH ROCK
NEW AFRICAN ADVENTURE
Now Open
ZSL
The Zoological Society of London (ZSL) is a charity devoted to the worldwide conservation of animals and their habitats. Registered Charity in England & Wales: no 208728
CHEETAH ROCK
Book online at zsl.org
Located off the M1 (J9)

the stables

The Laine Dankworth Centre
WAVENDON, MILTON KEYNES

Everyone knows The Stables, but did you know you can now enjoy a pre-show dinner here?

Open from 6pm on show nights, Café in2 enhances your evening by providing informal dining with real food made by a real chef, using fresh ingredients sourced from only the best local suppliers. Enjoy light tasty dishes, full on flavour but short on additives – and reasonably priced! Reservations: to avoid disappointment we recommend booking your table in advance. Contact the Box Office on 01908 280800 or email stables@stables.org.

With sell-out shows last season from chart stars Gabriella Cilmi and Beth Rowley, Soapstar Superstar's Richard Fleeshman and comedy from Lee Evans, Lenny Henry and Jo Brand, if you're not on The Stables' mailing list you could be missing out! Just £5 guarantees you'll be kept up-to-date with all our latest shows – call the Box Office for details.

Box Office: 01908 280800
Book online: www.stables.org
The Stables, Stockwell Lane, Wavendon, Milton Keynes MK17 8LU

THE FOODIE SQUARE GUIDE MAKES A PERFECT GIFT

- and still only £5

available from selected retailers throughout Beds, Bucks, Herts & Northants

or

ORDER DIRECT

from

www.thesquareguide.co.uk

THE FOODIE AWARD
2009

NOMINATE
YOUR FAVOURITE RESTAURANT
AND YOU COULD
WIN A MEAL FOR TWO!

We would like to hear from you, so nominate your favourite restaurant in Beds, Bucks, Herts or Northants for THE FOODIE Award. Just fill in the details below and send the form back to us. All forms returned to us by the closing date will be entered into a draw, the lucky winner of which will receive a meal for two at one of our four award winning restaurants.*

Please only nominate ONE establishment and take into consideration the quality of food, the service, the price and the surroundings before making your choice.

I would like to nominate: ______________________________ **for THE FOODIE Award**

because ____

____

Closing date for all nominations is 30th June 2009. (The winner of this years award will be published in the next edition of THE FOODIE Square Guide).

To be entered into the free draw please fill in your details below and then post back to:
THE FOODIE SQUARE GUIDE LIMITED, Nomination, 21 Hargreaves Nook, Blakelands, Milton Keynes MK14 5BS.

Name: ____

Address: ____

______________________________ **Postcode:** ________________

Telephone: ____________________ **Email:** ____________________

If you would like to be included to receive our free FOODIE Newsletter via email or post please tick the relevent box ☐ **email** ☐ **post**

*Terms and conditions apply. The meal for two is excluding drinks.

We only include restaurants in THE FOODIE Square Guide which have been recommended by *you*, so please keep sending in your comments and together we shall maintain the high standard you expect.

You can send your comments via email to: paul@thesquareguide.co.uk
or post to: THE FOODIE SQUARE GUIDE LTD, 21 Hargreaves Nook, Blakelands, Milton Keynes MK14 5BS

To enter the competition just fill in the answers to these two questions, both of which you will find in THE FOODIE Square Guide. Complete your details and post to the address below. The closing date for entries is 30th June 2009. Only one prize is available. Entries must be on the original form below. The winner will be the first correct entry to be drawn by the judges. The winners name will be published in the next edition of THE FOODIE Square Guide. The prize is a family ticket (2 adults and 2 children) for ZSL Whipsnade Zoo.
The lucky winner of last years prize was A. Marvin from Milton Keynes.

1. Which restaurant has a coat of arms with the inscription "GRATUS AD ORIS"? ....

2. What type of school is featured in Winslow? ....

Your details:-

Name: ....

Address: ....

Telephone: ....

Email: ....

Please post this entry back to: THE FOODIE Square Guide Ltd, 21 Hargreaves Nook, Blakelands, Milton Keynes MK14 5BS

The Foodie Voucher.
This voucher entitles the bearer on presentation to £5 discount.
Valid only at participating establishments displaying a GREEN £5 symbol on their advertisement within The Foodie.

counterfoil

The Foodie Voucher

This voucher entitles the bearer on presentation to £5 discount off final bill inclusive of VAT

Valid only at participating establishments displaying a GREEN £5 symbol
Valid until 30th September 2009

See terms and conditions overleaf

£5

The Foodie Voucher.
This voucher entitles the bearer on presentation to £5 discount.
Valid only at participating establishments displaying a GREEN £5 symbol on their advertisement within The Foodie.

counterfoil

The Foodie Voucher

This voucher entitles the bearer on presentation to £5 discount off final bill inclusive of VAT

Valid only at participating establishments displaying a GREEN £5 symbol
Valid until 30th September 2009

See terms and conditions overleaf

£5

The Foodie Voucher.
This voucher entitles the bearer on presentation to £5 discount.
Valid only at participating establishments displaying a GREEN £5 symbol on their advertisement within The Foodie.

counterfoil

The Foodie Voucher

This voucher entitles the bearer on presentation to £5 discount off final bill inclusive of VAT

Valid only at participating establishments displaying a GREEN £5 symbol
Valid until 30th September 2009

See terms and conditions overleaf

£5

Terms and Conditions

- The vouchers presented in this edition of The Foodie Square Guide are valid until 30th September 2009.
- Only one voucher may be redeemed against the final bill inclusive of VAT.
- The final bill inclusive of VAT must be to the value of £30.00 or more to qualify.
- The voucher is valid only in participating establishments which display the relevant voucher symbol on their display advert and with the participating establishment bearing the cost of the offer.
- The condition of the voucher on presentation and its acceptance is at the discretion of the participating establishment.
- No photocopy or any other reproduction of the voucher will be accepted.
- These vouchers may not be used in conjunction with any other offers.

IT MAY BE HELPFUL IF YOU MENTION THE USE OF THIS VOUCHER ***WHEN ORDERING*** YOUR MEAL

If you would like to be kept informed of any promotional offers from the establishment, please fill in your name and address below
Name
Address
Postcode Email
If you would not like your details passed on to any third parties please tick this box ❒

Terms and Conditions

- The vouchers presented in this edition of The Foodie Square Guide are valid until 30th September 2009.
- Only one voucher may be redeemed against the final bill inclusive of VAT.
- The final bill inclusive of VAT must be to the value of £30.00 or more to qualify.
- The voucher is valid only in participating establishments which display the relevant voucher symbol on their display advert and with the participating establishment bearing the cost of the offer.
- The condition of the voucher on presentation and its acceptance is at the discretion of the participating establishment.
- No photocopy or any other reproduction of the voucher will be accepted.
- These vouchers may not be used in conjunction with any other offers.

IT MAY BE HELPFUL IF YOU MENTION THE USE OF THIS VOUCHER ***WHEN ORDERING*** YOUR MEAL

If you would like to be kept informed of any promotional offers from the establishment, please fill in your name and address below
Name
Address
Postcode Email
If you would not like your details passed on to any third parties please tick this box ❒

Terms and Conditions

- The vouchers presented in this edition of The Foodie Square Guide are valid until 30th September 2009.
- Only one voucher may be redeemed against the final bill inclusive of VAT.
- The final bill inclusive of VAT must be to the value of £30.00 or more to qualify.
- The voucher is valid only in participating establishments which display the relevant voucher symbol on their display advert and with the participating establishment bearing the cost of the offer.
- The condition of the voucher on presentation and its acceptance is at the discretion of the participating establishment.
- No photocopy or any other reproduction of the voucher will be accepted.
- These vouchers may not be used in conjunction with any other offers.

IT MAY BE HELPFUL IF YOU MENTION THE USE OF THIS VOUCHER ***WHEN ORDERING*** YOUR MEAL

If you would like to be kept informed of any promotional offers from the establishment, please fill in your name and address below
Name
Address
Postcode Email
If you would not like your details passed on to any third parties please tick this box ❒

The Foodie Voucher.
This voucher entitles the bearer on presentation to 10% discount.
Valid only at participating establishments displaying a GOLD 10% symbol on their advertisement within The Foodie.

counterfoil

The Foodie Voucher

This voucher entitles the bearer on presentation to 10% discount off final bill inclusive of VAT

Valid only at participating establishments displaying a GOLD 10% symbol
Valid until 30th September 2009

See terms and conditions overleaf

The Foodie Voucher.
This voucher entitles the bearer on presentation to 10% discount.
Valid only at participating establishments displaying a GOLD 10% symbol on their advertisement within The Foodie.

counterfoil

The Foodie Voucher

This voucher entitles the bearer on presentation to 10% discount off final bill inclusive of VAT

Valid only at participating establishments displaying a GOLD 10% symbol
Valid until 30th September 2009

See terms and conditions overleaf

The Foodie Voucher.
This voucher entitles the bearer on presentation to 10% discount.
Valid only at participating establishments displaying a GOLD 10% symbol on their advertisement within The Foodie.

counterfoil

The Foodie Voucher

This voucher entitles the bearer on presentation to 10% discount off final bill inclusive of VAT

Valid only at participating establishments displaying a GOLD 10% symbol
Valid until 30th September 2009

See terms and conditions overleaf

10% 10% 10%

Terms and Conditions

- The vouchers presented in this edition of The Foodie Square Guide are valid until 30th September 2009.
- Only one voucher may be redeemed against the final bill inclusive of VAT.
- The final bill inclusive of VAT must be to the value of £30.00 or more to qualify.
- The voucher is valid only in participating establishments which display the relevant voucher symbol on their display advert and with the participating establishment bearing the cost of the offer.
- The condition of the voucher on presentation and its acceptance is at the discretion of the participating establishment.
- No photocopy or any other reproduction of the voucher will be accepted.
- These vouchers may not be used in conjunction with any other offers.

IT MAY BE HELPFUL IF YOU MENTION THE USE OF THIS VOUCHER ***WHEN ORDERING*** YOUR MEAL

If you would like to be kept informed of any promotional offers from the establishment, please fill in your name and address below

Name

Address

Postcode Email

If you would not like your details passed on to any third parties please tick this box ❒

Terms and Conditions

- The vouchers presented in this edition of The Foodie Square Guide are valid until 30th September 2009.
- Only one voucher may be redeemed against the final bill inclusive of VAT.
- The final bill inclusive of VAT must be to the value of £30.00 or more to qualify.
- The voucher is valid only in participating establishments which display the relevant voucher symbol on their display advert and with the participating establishment bearing the cost of the offer.
- The condition of the voucher on presentation and its acceptance is at the discretion of the participating establishment.
- No photocopy or any other reproduction of the voucher will be accepted.
- These vouchers may not be used in conjunction with any other offers.

IT MAY BE HELPFUL IF YOU MENTION THE USE OF THIS VOUCHER ***WHEN ORDERING*** YOUR MEAL

If you would like to be kept informed of any promotional offers from the establishment, please fill in your name and address below

Name

Address

Postcode Email

If you would not like your details passed on to any third parties please tick this box ❒

Terms and Conditions

- The vouchers presented in this edition of The Foodie Square Guide are valid until 30th September 2009.
- Only one voucher may be redeemed against the final bill inclusive of VAT.
- The final bill inclusive of VAT must be to the value of £30.00 or more to qualify.
- The voucher is valid only in participating establishments which display the relevant voucher symbol on their display advert and with the participating establishment bearing the cost of the offer.
- The condition of the voucher on presentation and its acceptance is at the discretion of the participating establishment.
- No photocopy or any other reproduction of the voucher will be accepted.
- These vouchers may not be used in conjunction with any other offers.

IT MAY BE HELPFUL IF YOU MENTION THE USE OF THIS VOUCHER ***WHEN ORDERING*** YOUR MEAL

If you would like to be kept informed of any promotional offers from the establishment, please fill in your name and address below

Name

Address

Postcode Email

If you would not like your details passed on to any third parties please tick this box ❒

The Foodie Voucher.
This voucher entitles the bearer on presentation to one bottle of house wine.
Valid only at participating establishments displaying a SILVER BOTTLE symbol on their advertisement within The Foodie.

counterfoil

The Foodie Voucher

This voucher entitles the bearer on presentation to one bottle of house wine

Valid only at participating establishments displaying a SILVER BOTTLE symbol

Valid until 30th September 2009

See terms and conditions overleaf

The Foodie Voucher.
This voucher entitles the bearer on presentation to one bottle of house wine.
Valid only at participating establishments displaying a SILVER BOTTLE symbol on their advertisement within The Foodie.

counterfoil

The Foodie Voucher

This voucher entitles the bearer on presentation to one bottle of house wine

Valid only at participating establishments displaying a SILVER BOTTLE symbol

Valid until 30th September 2009

See terms and conditions overleaf

The Foodie Voucher.
This voucher entitles the bearer on presentation to one bottle of house wine.
Valid only at participating establishments displaying a SILVER BOTTLE symbol on their advertisement within The Foodie.

counterfoil

The Foodie Voucher

This voucher entitles the bearer on presentation to one bottle of house wine

Valid only at participating establishments displaying a SILVER BOTTLE symbol

Valid until 30th September 2009

See terms and conditions overleaf

Terms and Conditions

- The vouchers presented in this edition of The Foodie Square Guide are valid until 30th September 2009.
- Only one voucher may be redeemed against the final bill inclusive of VAT.
- The final bill inclusive of VAT must be to the value of £30.00 or more to qualify.
- The voucher is valid only in participating establishments which display the relevant voucher symbol on their display advert and with the participating establishment bearing the cost of the offer.
- The condition of the voucher on presentation and its acceptance is at the discretion of the participating establishment.
- No photocopy or any other reproduction of the voucher will be accepted.
- These vouchers may not be used in conjunction with any other offers.

IT MAY BE HELPFUL IF YOU MENTION THE USE OF THIS VOUCHER ***WHEN ORDERING*** YOUR MEAL

If you would like to be kept informed of any promotional offers from the establishment, please fill in your name and address below
Name
Address
Postcode Email
If you would not like your details passed on to any third parties please tick this box ❐

Terms and Conditions

- The vouchers presented in this edition of The Foodie Square Guide are valid until 30th September 2009.
- Only one voucher may be redeemed against the final bill inclusive of VAT.
- The final bill inclusive of VAT must be to the value of £30.00 or more to qualify.
- The voucher is valid only in participating establishments which display the relevant voucher symbol on their display advert and with the participating establishment bearing the cost of the offer.
- The condition of the voucher on presentation and its acceptance is at the discretion of the participating establishment.
- No photocopy or any other reproduction of the voucher will be accepted.
- These vouchers may not be used in conjunction with any other offers.

IT MAY BE HELPFUL IF YOU MENTION THE USE OF THIS VOUCHER ***WHEN ORDERING*** YOUR MEAL

If you would like to be kept informed of any promotional offers from the establishment, please fill in your name and address below
Name
Address
Postcode Email
If you would not like your details passed on to any third parties please tick this box ❐

Terms and Conditions

- The vouchers presented in this edition of The Foodie Square Guide are valid until 30th September 2009.
- Only one voucher may be redeemed against the final bill inclusive of VAT.
- The final bill inclusive of VAT must be to the value of £30.00 or more to qualify.
- The voucher is valid only in participating establishments which display the relevant voucher symbol on their display advert and with the participating establishment bearing the cost of the offer.
- The condition of the voucher on presentation and its acceptance is at the discretion of the participating establishment.
- No photocopy or any other reproduction of the voucher will be accepted.
- These vouchers may not be used in conjunction with any other offers.

IT MAY BE HELPFUL IF YOU MENTION THE USE OF THIS VOUCHER ***WHEN ORDERING*** YOUR MEAL

If you would like to be kept informed of any promotional offers from the establishment, please fill in your name and address below
Name
Address
Postcode Email
If you would not like your details passed on to any third parties please tick this box ❐

the complete series

5 INGREDIENTS

hinkler

Published by Hinkler Books Pty Ltd
45–55 Fairchild Street
Heatherton Victoria 3202 Australia
www.hinkler.com.au

hinkler

Cover design: Hinkler Design Studio
Typesetting: MPS Limited
Prepress: Graphic Print Group

ISBN: 978 1 7430 8639 1

Printed and bound in China

Contents

Introduction......4

Breakfast......7

Dips & sauces......31

Seafood, poultry & meat......55

Pasta & rice......123

Vegetarian......147

Desserts......167

Weights & measures......188

Index......190

Introduction

With our busy modern lifestyles, we often have little time for the preparation and cooking of the family meal. To deal with this problem, this cookbook has been produced using the minimum of ingredients and with recipes designed to be tasty, easy to prepare and quick to cook.

In order to make these recipes as tasty as possible using only five ingredients, our chefs have used some commercially available sauces and spices, all chosen to make the best possible meal with the minimum of fuss.

Long before modern cooking, our ancestors trapped and killed game and most probably ate it raw as they stripped the meat off the carcasses.

Somewhere in the distant past, fire was introduced, and our ancestors became adept at cooking their kill on a stick over an open fire.

Some adventurous forerunners of the modern cook then found that with the addition of some plants, leaves and roots they could enhance the flavour of their meal.

As civilisation progressed so did our cooking skills, so today we find that some gourmet recipes can have as many as 40 ingredients, and can take days to prepare and cook – totally impractical for most people.

While often looking to reduce our household costs, we certainly don't want to reduce the nutrition and taste of the meals we put on the table.

Our chefs and home economists have accepted the challenge to make tasty, nutritious, easy-to-prepare meals using the minimum of ingredients, and have produced this book full of great recipes using only five ingredients. We have not included salt in our ingredient lists, as we find that it is used by everyone in a different manner – from none at all to excessive amounts.

You should also have a reasonably well-stocked larder of herbs and spices, plus a selection of sauces – again, these can be used to suit the individual palate. Look through the displays in your local supermarket and choose a range that will suit your tastes.

While putting together a five-ingredient cookbook is essentially not very difficult, making a five-ingredient recipe that will satisfy all members of the family most definitely is.

We are assisted by the huge number of processed foods available at your supermarket, including sauces, jams (jellies), chutneys, mustards and canned or frozen fish, meat and vegetables.

We have broken the recipes up into chapters to make it easy to select the recipe you need for a particular occasion. We cover great breakfasts; entertaining dips and sauces; seafood, poultry and meat for any occasion; pasta and rice; vegetarian dishes and some terrific desserts.

BREAKFAST